Seeing The HiddEn Minority

Increasing the Talent Pool Through Identity, Socialization, and Mentoring Constructs

Contemporary Perspectives on Access, Equity and Achievement

Series Editor

Chance W. Lewis
University of North Carolina at Charlotte

Contemporary Perspectives on Access, Equity, and Achievement

Chance W. Lewis, Editor

Seeing The HiddEn Minority: Increasing the Talent Pool Through Identity, Socialization, and Mentoring Constructs (2020)
edited by Andrea L. Tyler, Stephen D. Hancock, and Sonyia C. Richardson

Conquering Academia: Transparent Experiences of Diverse Female Doctoral Students (2019)
edited by Sonyia C. Richardson and Chance W. Lewis

Community College Teacher Preparation for Diverse Geographies: Implications for Access and Equity for Preparing a Diverse Teacher Workforce (2019)
edited by Mark M. D'Amico and Chance W. Lewis

Global Perspectives of Issues and Solutions in Urban Education (2019)
edited by Petra A. Robinson, Ayana Allen-Handy, Amber Bryant, and Chance W. Lewis

Let's Stop Calling It an Achievement Gap: How Public Education in the United States Maintains Disparate Educational Experiences for Students of Color (2019)
by Autumn A. Arnett

Responding to the Call for Educational Justice: Transformative Catholic-Led Initiatives in Urban Education (2019)
edited by L. Mickey Fenzel and Melodie Wyttenbach

Recruiting, Retaining, and Engaging African American Males at Selective Public Research Universities: Challenges and Opportunities in Academics and Sports (2018)
edited by Louis A. Castenell, Tarek C. Grantham, and Billy J. Hawkins

Advancing Equity and Diversity in Student Affairs: A Festschrift in Honor of Melvin C. Terrell (2017)
edited by Jerlando F. L. Jackson, LaVar J. Charleston, and Cornelius K. Gilbert

Cultivating Achievement, Respect, and Empowerment (CARE) for African American Girls in Pre-K–12 Settings: Implications for Access, Equity and Achievement (2016)
edited by Patricia J. Larke, Gwendolyn Webb-Hasan, and Jemimah L. Young

(List continues on next page)

Reaching the Mountaintop of the Academy: Personal Narratives, Advice and Strategies From Black Distinguished and Endowed Professors (2015)
edited by Gail L. Thompson, Fred A. Bonner, II, and Chance W. Lewis

Priorities of the Professoriate: Engaging Multiple Forms of Scholarship Across Rural and Urban Institutions (2015)
edited by Fred A. Bonner, II, Rosa M. Banda,
Petra A. Robinson, Chance W. Lewis, and Barbara Lofton

Autoethnography as a Lighthouse: Illuminating Race, Research, and the Politics of Schooling (2015)
edited by Stephen Hancock, Ayana Allen, and Chance W. Lewis

Teacher Education and Black Communities: Implications for Access, Equity and Achievement (2014)
edited by Yolanda Sealey-Ruiz, Chance W. Lewis, and Ivory Toldson

Improving Urban Schools: Equity and Access in K–16 STEM Education (2013)
edited by Mary Margaret Capraro,
Robert M. Capraro, and Chance W. Lewis

Black Males in Postsecondary Education: Examining their Experiences in Diverse Institutional Contexts (2012)
edited by Adriel A. Hilton, J. Luke Wood, and Chance W. Lewis

Yes We Can! Improving Urban Schools through Innovative Educational Reform (2011)
edited by Leanne L. Howell, Chance W. Lewis, and Norvella Carter

Seeing The HiddEn Minority
Increasing the Talent Pool Through Identity, Socialization, and Mentoring Constructs

edited by

Andrea L. Tyler
Tennessee State University

**Stephen D. Hancock
and Sonyia C. Richardson**
The University of North Carolina at Charlotte

INFORMATION AGE PUBLISHING, INC.
Charlotte, NC • www.infoagepub.com

Library of Congress Cataloging-in-Publication Data

CIP record for this book is available from the Library of Congress
http://www.loc.gov

ISBNs: 978-1-64113-948-9 (Paperback)

           978-1-64113-949-6 (Hardcover)

           978-1-64113-950-2 (ebook)

Copyright © 2020 Information Age Publishing Inc.

All rights reserved. No part of this publication may be reproduced, stored in a retrieval system, or transmitted, in any form or by any means, electronic, mechanical, photocopying, microfilming, recording or otherwise, without written permission from the publisher.

Printed in the United States of America

CONTENTS

Preface .... *ix*

Acknowledgments .... *xi*
    Andrea L. Tyler

SECTION I: SOCIALIZATION

1. Using the Frameworks of Socialization and Acculturation to
Understand the Trajectory of Scientists of Color
Karri A. Holley and Joretta Joseph *3*

2. Strategies for Using Critical Systems Theory to Support
Socialization of Undergraduate African American Students
in STEM
Sonyia C. Richardson and Lenora Crabtree *17*

SECTION II: MENTORING

3. Mentoring for STEM Advocacy
Cameron Denson and Tamecia R. Jones *39*

4. Different Worlds: A Picture of STEM Mentorships
at PWIs and HBCUs
Daniel Alston and Brandi Copeland-Kamp *63*

5. STEM Doctoral Student Degree Attainment: How Demands,
Structures, and Networks Impact Timely Degree Completion
Carrie Klein and Hironao Okahana *83*

viii CONTENTS

SECTION III: IDENTITY

6. The Role of Identity on Persistence for Black Women
    Doctoral Students in Science
    Andrea L. Tyler, Letimicia Fears, and Monica L. Miles 101

7. Strengthening STEM Identities: Combatting Curriculum
    Trauma in African American Students
    Stephen D. Hancock and Michelle B. Pass 121

8. Unearthing Factors That Contribute to Distorted Science
    Identities in African American Women
    Ansley Booker 133

AFTERWORD

9. Strengthening Identities to Combat Marginalization:
    Recurring Themes and Implications
    Stephen D. Hancock and Sonyia C. Richardson 147

About the Contributors...153

PREFACE

This book is the lens through which readers can understand and address the challenges faced by Black students in science, technology, engineering, and mathematics (STEM). This knowledge begins with understanding the complexities they [Black STEM students] face at all levels of education. A sense of urgency is now needed to explore these complexities and how they impact students at all educational levels. This book will explore *hidden figures* and concerns of social connectedness, mentoring practices, and identity constructs that uncover unnoticed talent pools and encourage STEM matriculation among Black STEM students' in pre-K–12 and post-secondary landscapes.

Each author in this book attempts to reconfirm the participation of Black students in STEM fields, is an issue of national concern. Educators and policymakers are seeking to promote STEM studies and eventual degree attainment, especially those from underrepresented groups, including Black students, women, economically disadvantaged, and students with disabilities. Literature shows that this has been of great interest to researchers, policymakers, and institutions for several years (Nettles & Millet, 2006; Council of Graduate School (CGS), 2009; National Science Foundation (NSF), 2006), therefore an extensive understanding of access, attrition, and degree completion for Black students in STEM is needed.

Seeing The HiddEn Minority, pp. ix–x
Copyright © 2020 by Information Age Publishing
All rights of reproduction in any form reserved.

x PREFACE

OUTLINE OF THIS BOOK

This book comprises nine chapter across three sections focusing on STEM monitoring, identity, and socialization across the PK–20 context. This book can be read by two distinctive groups, those within the STEM research domain and those outside the domain.

SECTION 1: Socialization

Social discourse concerning how male and females are supposed to enact their socially sanctioned roles is being played out daily in educational institutions. Individuals who chose STEM education and STEM careers are constantly battling this social discourse. It is necessary for P–20 STEM spaces to examine and integrate understanding of socialization within the larger societal culture for systemic and lasting change to happen.

SECTION 1: Mentoring

Mentoring is a nurturing process in which a more skilled or more experienced person, serving as a role model teaches, sponsors, encourages, counsels, and befriends a less skilled or less experienced person for the purpose of promoting the latter's academic, professional and/or personal development.

SECTION 1: Identity

Research focusing on identity constructs in STEM has become more common, especially as it relates to student retention and attrition. Researchers have been able to use identity as a way to examine how social stigma can cause students to (dis)identify within STEM spaces.

We hope this book is widely read by educators (PK–20), policymakers, and those interested in changing the dominate narrative that speaks to the "hidden" aspects of STEM and STEM education.

ACKNOWLEDGMENTS

Andrea L. Tyler

I thank God from whom all my blessing flow.... I thank Him for His grace and mercy and for being the guiding light on my path through life.

This book was made possible by all the contributions to my personal and professional life. I am deeply grateful to my family and close friends for creating a productive and supporting climate to work within. Without their support and encouragement, this book would have been impossible. I especially want to thank my children, Marques and Naylah, for their unconditional love and support. I love you around the world and back again, forever and a day. My children have seen and experienced, firsthand, my quest for education and this book. I have always wanted to set an example of excellence in education and life for them; and I pray that I have done just that. I would also like to thank my mother, Nancy Tyler-Brown for all her support and encouragement on this journey.

I am grateful to my lifelong mentors; Drs. Sally Lloyd, Jhan Berry, Sonja Lanehart; and Stephen D. Hancock. I am deeply grateful for their advice throughout the years on my educational walk, my scholarship, and the inspiration for this book. Over the years our conversations about my research have been engaging, stimulating and fostered discussions that brought this book to fruition. Under their mentoring and guidance I began to (re)shape my research agenda focusing on the experiences of Black

---

Seeing The HiddEn Minority, pp. xi–xii
Copyright © 2020 by Information Age Publishing
All rights of reproduction in any form reserved.

STEM students in higher education; specially focusing on identity constructs, mentorship, graduate education. and career pathways. It is without saying that I would not be where I am today without their support.

EDITORS' COLLECTIVE ACKNOWLEDGMENTS

We are grateful to many people for their roles in helping this project to completion, but we send a special thanks to each author that contributed to this book. Each author brought a unique approach to the topic of STEM mentoring, identity, and socialization. This book project journey has been rewarding and informative and we thank you for your insight, scholarship, and collaboration.

We also thank the Series Editor, Dr. Chance W. Lewis, the Carol Grotnes Belk Distinguished Professor and Endowed Chair of Urban Education at the University of North Carolina at Charlotte, for his insight, vision, and support of this book.

Finally, we thank the executive editor of Information Age Publishing for providing support and patience of this book project.

SECTION I

SOCIALIZATION

CHAPTER 1

USING THE FRAMEWORKS OF SOCIALIZATION AND ACCULTURATION TO UNDERSTAND THE TRAJECTORY OF SCIENTISTS OF COLOR

Karri A. Holley
The University of Alabama

Joretta Joseph
University of Southern California

Numerous efforts to diversify the STEM-education pipeline have occurred over the past decades. These efforts target different segments of the education system, including K–12 education, undergraduate education, and graduate education. The intent of racial-ethnic diversification efforts across the education pipeline is to increase the number of scientists of color to better reflect the overall U.S. population and embrace the full potential of the country's capacity for producing scientific research. Women of color, for example, are underrepresented in STEM-degree completion rates when compared to the percentage of minority female U.S. citizens

Seeing The HiddEn Minority, pp. 3–16
Copyright © 2020 by Information Age Publishing
All rights of reproduction in any form reserved.

(Ong, Smith, & Ko, 2018), while Black men accounted for only 4% of students enrolled in undergraduate engineering programs (Strayhorn, 2015). However, despite numerous efforts on an institutional and policy level, diversity levels among STEM professionals overall show marginal and uneven growth, raising questions about how to best encourage young scientists of color to pursue and persist in STEM careers. Using conceptual frameworks of socialization and acculturation, this chapter explores the pipeline into graduate STEM programs for scientists of color and their experiences once enrolled.

The chapter is structured into three parts. First, we reflect on existing data and empirical research that demonstrates how students of color engage in STEM-related learning, with a specific emphasis on the role of the undergraduate institution, undergraduate faculty, and the transition to graduate and doctoral education. After a brief overview of constructs related to socialization and acculturation, we offer ideas as to how student interactions before graduate study shape academic development and future professional trajectories. We conclude with suggestions for research and practice, including (1) how conceptual frameworks might be expanded to better understand the experiences of scientists of color and (2) lessons for all academic institutions related to encouraging more students of color to enter STEM fields. Our goal is to summarize the current state of research and practice related to graduate students of color in STEM fields, and to provide ideas for understanding future trajectories.

Summary of student demographics and programs. Educational experiences before college graduation provide either a foundation or a deterrent for future STEM-related pursuits. Maltese and Tai (2011) found that the greatest loss of interest from students in STEM careers comes between high school graduation and undergraduate matriculation. Further, students who complete more rigorous high school level coursework are more likely to pursue STEM careers compared to their peers. This association can be problematic for women and students of color. While female high school students take more advanced coursework than male students, they are less likely to complete the highest level of the course. Black and Hispanic students were much less likely to complete advanced coursework than White or Asian peers (Maltese & Tai, 2011). The completion of high school mathematics courses and maintaining a positive attitude towards mathematics are important factors for students to select STEM majors; similar trends exist for courses in the sciences. Many students who major in STEM-fields make decisions about their choice of major before high school graduation (Maltese & Tai, 2011), emphasizing the importance not only of a college preparatory high school curriculum, but also exposure to different career options.

Data from the National Center for Education Statistics (2013) illustrate that 28% of bachelor's degree students and 20% of associate's degree students entered into a STEM-related major; biology is the most common major, while mathematics and physical science are the least common. Not all of these students persist in the major until degree completion. Approximately half of those who decide to major in a STEM-related field at a four-year institution change their major or drop out of the institution before degree completion. Similar to findings of Maltese and Tai (2011), the NCES data demonstrate the crucial role of mathematics courses early in the postsecondary curriculum, reinforcing how K–12 preparation (or lack thereof) can influence a student's postsecondary trajectory. Women earn more than half of the STEM-related bachelor's degrees awarded in the United States, and have for almost two decades (National Science Foundation [NSF], 2018); the distribution of degrees among various racial-ethnic groups remains disproportionate, with the share of degrees earned by white U.S. citizens and permanent residents at 63% (NSF, 2018).

Broadly, the efforts to increase and sustain diversity in the STEM pipeline focuses on the key elements indicated by data as crucial preparatory experiences, moments of knowledge acquisition, or turning points. In K–12 education, these elements center on precollege programs; mentoring; and curriculum reform and development, while in postsecondary education, attention is given to academic support; professional development; mentoring; and faculty development. Several programs have emerged as models for other academic institutions. Programs at minority serving institutions, such as Historically Black Colleges and Universities (HBCUs), Tribal Colleges, or Hispanic Serving Institutions (HSIs) draw from a campus climate supportive of the achievements of minority students across all disciplines to specifically target engagement and persistence in STEM-related fields. The Meyerhoff Scholars Program at the University of Maryland, Baltimore County is considered one of the strongest models; the program combines financial and academic support as well as faculty, family, and community involvement (Maton, Pollard, Weise, & Hrabowski, 2012). Connecting elements across the student experience underscores how the involvement of multiple stakeholders helps facilitate student success. Programs focused on undergraduate students that prepare students to make the transition to graduate programs and engage in research practice are noted in Table 1.1 (Graham, 2013).

Graduate education is crucial to preparing faculty and scholars for the future. Graduate school education also contributes highly skilled workers that compete globally in industry, academia, and a research based economy (NSF, 2014), and is seen as key to the advanced knowledge necessary to develop a robust professional trajectory in STEM-related fields. The transition from undergraduate to graduate education illustrates the importance

Table 1.1.
Predoctorate STEM Programs

Program	Partnering Schools	Target Disciplines	Program Components
Bridges to the Doctorate Program	Alcorn State University and Pennsylvania State University	Veterinary and biomedical sciences	Stipend, tuition benefits, mentorship, shared curriculum
Master's to PhD Bridge program	Fisk University and Vanderbilt University	Physics, astronomy, material science	Financial support, mentorship, shared research opportunities, support groups
HBCU-UP ACE (funded by NSF, at multiple locations)	Southern A&M University and Beijing Forestry University, Oak Ridge Laboratories	Sustainable materials, energy, technology	Collaborative research opportunities, internships, international collaboration
UC-HBCU Initiative	Florida A&M University and University of California, Santa Barbara	Education, evaluation, assessment	Financial support, travel support, mentorship, research opportunities
Yale-Bouchet Conference	Yale University	Across disciplines including STEM fields	Engagement with other graduate students and research opportunities
Delta Program	University of Wisconsin	Various STEM fields	Hands on research, student support and engagement with other students, post docs and faculty, and research opportunities
APS Physics Bridge Program	Current Bridge Sites: California State University —Long Beach, Florida State University, Indiana University, the Ohio State University, University of South Florida, and University of Central Florida	Physics	Mentoring to and through their doctoral program and research opportunities
Bridge to PhD	Columbia University	Natural sciences	Research, coursework and mentoring
Physics Bridge Program	MIT	Physics	Mentoring, course work, and mentoring
Imes-Moore Bridge Program	University of Michigan	Physics	Financial support, mentoring, and research opportunities

of faculty engagement and mentoring with students of color, with the understanding that students have unique experiences shaped by their individual identities and interests. Further, acknowledging multiple and overlapping identities is crucial. Women of color experience gender and racial bias "situating them in a unique position of confronting multiple systems of oppression" (Ong, Wright, Espinosa, & Orfield, 2011, p. 182). Since women do not always pursue graduate degrees in STEM at the same rate as their male counterparts (Myers & Pavel, 2011), the influence of these multiple systems of oppression are especially significant.

In 2010, working with partner research universities, the Council of Graduate Schools (CGS) sought to identify strategies that would increase doctoral degree completion, particularly among underrepresented students. These strategies reinforced those from existing literature on undergraduate and graduate student success, including mentoring and advising, financial support, program environment, and research experiences (CGS, 2010).

"Success in achieving a PhD depends upon a close and effective working relationship with one's advisor and mentor," the CGS concluded (2010, p. 33). For students of color from diverse backgrounds, finding a supportive advisor and mentor in graduate education is a frequent challenge. In addition, because of the need to facilitate a match between scholarly and intellectual interests, this challenge might be in part due to the lack of diversity among graduate faculty in STEM-related fields, especially those at predominantly White institutions (Johnson, Jones, Haddad, Wilcox, & Wilcox, 2016), or from a student's transition from a minority serving institution to a predominantly White institution (Joseph, 2013). Navigating the program environment might also be difficult for diverse students. Graduate students experience their disciplinary program of study as part of numerous educational levels, such as the individual research laboratory, the academic program or department, and the academic institution more broadly. The perception of a chilly climate or an environment that does not recognize the needs of a diverse student population can have a negative influence (Ong et al., 2011).

Ampaw and Jaeger (2011) documented that minority students are less likely to complete their doctoral degrees compared to White students. For minority students, the development stage, or the time of their degree program when students are expected to develop a research agenda, can be problematic. "Students of color seek coherence in their research topic and cultural identity" (p. 654), Ampaw and Jaeger concluded, which potentially "affects the way they participate and engage in the institutional experience."

Financial support is also an important contributor to degree persistence and degree completion for students of color. Receiving financial support throughout doctoral enrollment can accelerate the time to degree, although not all financial support has the same effect (Ampaw & Jaeger, 2011). Students who hold research assistantships in STEM-related fields have a shorter time to degree compared to their peers who hold teaching assistantships, and questions remain over whether minority graduate students hold research positions at the same rate as their non-minority peers (de Valero, 2001).

Ultimately, when considering the success of students of color that go on to achieve doctorate degrees in STEM-related fields, dedicated faculty who serve as role models, advisors, and mentors combined with student research experiences, a supportive program environment, and financial support remain crucial elements. The lack of these elements emphasizes the need for academic institutions to continue to devote efforts towards developing and supporting a diverse graduate student pipeline.

Theories of socialization and acculturation. The experiences of students of color in STEM fields are commonly examined through socialization theory, and less commonly through theories of acculturation. "Socialization in graduate school refers to the processes through which individuals gain the knowledge, skills, and values necessary for successful entry into a professional career requiring an advanced level of specialized knowledge and skills," wrote Weidman, Twale, and Stein (2001, p. iii). Through investment, involvement, and the acquisition of knowledge, students acquire community membership. These communities of practice provide examples of linguistic, cognitive, and behavior norms. For example, doctoral students might participate in the annual conference of the discipline's primary organization, or publish in discipline-specific journals. Further, socialization requires "an interpretive process of creating meanings to make sense of an organization through [a student's] own unique backgrounds and the current contexts" (Azizova & Felder, 2017, p. 147) The cumulative nature of socialization suggests that all educational experiences matter, not just those in graduate school, although the sequence of events and a student's perception of them vary depending on numerous characteristics (Weidman et al., 2001).

The first element, knowledge acquisition, occurs when students develop fluency in the language, culture, and ideology of the community. Doing so shapes their professional identity, and allows them to act as experienced role incumbents. While the acquisition of formal, field-specific content knowledge is included, so is acquiring tacit, implicit knowledge related to role functions, norms, and beliefs. The second element, investment, requires students to eliminate other options in their pursuit of community membership. By devoting time, energy, and money into the field as well as cultivating a sense of obligation to other community members, students gradually come to see their professional (and oftentimes, personal) identity congruent with the community. The final element, involvement, requires students to interact with faculty and other senior community members as well as their peers. This involvement typically occurs through professional activities such as attending conferences or workshops, but can also be seen through conducting research and writing manuscripts. Becoming involved in the community allows students to see the inner workings of the community as well as understand how their own behavior can be aligned with community norms and values.

Socialization is a highly individualized experience dependent on the student and the institutional context. Its nature as a social process defined by interactions between people as well as interactions between students and the university mean that minority students may be disadvantaged during their doctoral curriculum. Opportunities to connect with program faculty regarding research, including conference presentations and publications, may feel limited for students who struggle to connect with a primary advisor, while students who pursue the degree part-time or work off campus may be disadvantaged in terms of time. The nature of knowledge and the perceived priorities of academia matter—for example, Thoman, Muragishi, and Smith (2017) illustrated how minority students in STEM fields found motivation through a prosocial research culture, or one defined by the belief that research and knowledge production hold social value and would benefit larger society. Investment in a diverse scientific workforce requires recognition of the different epistemological and ontological perspectives scientists bring to their work.

Related to ideas of socialization are those of acculturation. Acculturation occurs when individuals adopt and integrate traits, values, and behaviors that belong to another group (Joseph, 2014). Most frequently, this process occurs when members of minority groups adopt traits perceived to be associated with a dominant group. For students of color entering postsecondary education, the perceived need to achieve cultural congruity (or a match with the values perceived to be normative to the academic institution, or those associated with middle to upper income White students) can slow development and academic advancement. A potential result of this interaction for the student might be psychological distress, low academic grades, or dropping out of the institution. Chun and colleagues (2016) documented cultural congruity as a significant predictor of psychological wellbeing among minority students as well as a predictor of students' grade point average.

Acculturation is also experienced when students try to maintain membership in multiple cultures; that is, rather than wholly adopting the traits perceived to be associated with a dominant group, they seek to adopt these traits while at the same time retaining the traits of their home culture. The balance inherent to this act is a difficult one. For example, students who do not speak English as a first-language might experience discomfort related to their language skills, while others might find it difficult to travel between the campus environment and their home/family environment (Chun et al., 2016). For students enrolled in doctoral programs, acquiring the skills prioritized by their academic setting may highlight this conflict, especially if the students are transitioning from undergraduate studies at a minority serving institution to graduate education at a predominantly White or diverse institution (Joseph, 2014). Understanding acculturation requires understanding relationships, not just between students and faculty as well as students and peers, but also between students and their home communities.

Socialization and acculturation are not neutral phenomena. Inherent to each process is a give-and-take relationship where the student may feel they are giving more than they are receiving, or where they are put in a disadvantaged position related to their academic career. Individual demographics, such as race, ethnicity, gender, and income level, shape how students engage in these experiences. Race has wide-reaching implications for building knowledge and facilitating student success (Felder, Stevenson, & Gasman, 2014). Race holds longstanding significance related to education because "students are educated in distinct racial contexts" (Hurtado, Clayton-Perderson, Milem, & Allen, 1998, p. 282), meaning that race shapes student outcomes well before they reach the stage of doctoral education. Ultimately, perceptions of race have the potential to be a key element of (or detriment to) academic success (Felder et al., 2014). This perception explains the importance of students of color engaging with faculty and administrators who reflect their personal demographic. Seeing role models in professional positions who have successfully navigated complex issues of socialization and acculturation influences the student's level of commitment and willingness to engage in the personal and professional tasks inherent to graduate work (Herzig, 2004).

Not only do students need to demonstrate effort and grasp necessary skills and knowledge, but they also need to navigate the context of the department and understand the values and expectations that influence their success (Amenkhienan & Kogan, 2004). Engagement with departmental cultures as part of the graduate student socialization or acculturation process potentially represents one of the primary reasons for high attrition for doctoral students of color (Joseph, 2014). A student's success in doctoral education is a reflection of understanding the external and internal policies of the department, institutional values, and traditions as well as what is perceived to be acceptable, normal, and "high reward" behavior for the academic discipline (Herzig, 2004). These perceptions vary not just based on individual demographics, but also previous educational experiences and expectations entering the graduate school environment.

One challenge for graduate students of color in STEM-related fields is that they may be the only student of color in the program, or one of only a handful of students who represent "difference" in terms of the departmental or institutional culture, causing feelings of stress and isolation. In graduate programs, students are also expected to connect with a faculty member (as an advisor and mentor) from the onset. This connection is critical to ensure ample time to develop a good working relationship, which is essential to student persistence (Holley & Caldwell, 2012). A supportive environment, where there is a common understanding of the program and the expectations, increases the persistence and success of doctoral students of color.

Suggestions for research and practice. Pursuing a graduate education (doctorate degree) is a major undertaking. Such a task comes with risk and few guarantees of academic or professional success. The sense of risk-taking can be heightened by the individual and unique way that students experience the program as well as their evolution into a scholar and colleague (Holley & Caldwell, 2012). A student's personal and professional identity results from a multitude of perspectives, not just their own unique demographics, but also based on the conditions and circumstances within their institutions and a myriad of aforementioned matters (Ibarra, 2001). This overlapping process is of particular interest since identity, in an academic setting, is based on the student's interpretations of their mastery of skills, behavior, interactions with others, encouragement of capabilities, and prior academic achievement (Phinney, Horenczyk, Lieband, & Vedder, 2001).

Higher education, particularly doctoral education, continues to be a vehicle of social capital (Felder, 2015). At its most basic level social capital allows people to make choices beyond their perceived limits within society. This social capital is a sum of social trust and informal associative networks (Lappe & Dubois, 1997), and can be a critical factor in students' success. For example, networks developed during a student's undergraduate years can carry forward into graduate and doctoral programs. While the undergraduate institution is not the only factor in a graduate student's success, these networks contribute to the student experience. Given the history of racial exclusion in American higher education, students of color could only attend Historically Black Colleges and Universities in numbers that would amount to a critical mass (Felder & Freeman, 2016). As recent of 2015, according to the NSF (2018) data, 13.3% of African Americans enrolled in graduate science and engineering programs attended a HBCU. In addition, 30% of all African Americans who attained doctorate degrees in engineering and science in 2012 have baccalaureate origins at a HBCU—despite the fact that many HBCUs do not offer doctorate programs or even have defined programs that are geared to preparing students for graduate education. The steady numbers of HBCU graduates who go on to pursue

STEM graduate degrees at non-institutions emphasize the beneficial ways the HBCU culture shapes students and also how academic and professional networks can work on multiple levels to influence the student trajectory.

Preparing undergraduate students of color for graduate education before they apply is beneficial to their success, including research opportunities and faculty interactions (Ko, Kachchaf, Hodari, & Ong, 2014). This level of engagement allows the student to build a knowledge base and foster the sort of social capital likely valued within a graduate program (Felder et al., 2014). Giving undergraduate students the opportunity to participate in programs that offer a "sense of community" and treating students in a supportive and fair manner helps build confidence as well as practical and professional skills (Ko et al., 2014). This sense of community in various spaces, including institutional spaces, social spaces, and counter spaces, contribute to the student's sense of belonging (Ong et al., 2018). Such spaces may be vital to a student of color's decision to stay at critical points in their matriculation (Joseph, 2014).

A challenge inherent to socialization and acculturation theories is the idea that students of color must acclimate to the institutional norm in order to be academic successful, including denouncing racial and ethnic identities as well as disassociating with like peers (Marsh, 2013). For example, traditional socialization theory assumes a norm that reflects the majority of community members—in an academic department, research laboratory, or academic discipline, this presumed norm may not reflect the identities of students of color. By dismissing an individual's personal preferences, expressions, and other influences that make up a person's racial identity, students may decide to leave an unwelcoming academic program (Marsh, 2013).

Students of color with a strong sense of self-identity rooted in individual identity characteristics such as race, ethnicity, and gender, have high aspirations and achieve at high academic levels (Marsh, 2013). This strong sense of self and achievement is also enhanced when students of color maintain connections with those individuals that support who they are, as people and scholars (Joseph, 2007). Students of color do not possess a singular identity, but rather an identity associated with more than one group (such as gender, race/ethnicity, and nationality) with both positive and negative thoughts about one or all of these groups (Settles, 2006). These thoughts might include pleasure, cultural pride, and the desire to connect with others who share similar identity characteristics. In order to account for the multiple identities that define an individual, graduate programs should consider how the educational process, both formally and informally, allows space for student identities and celebration of diversity throughout the progress towards degree (Joseph, 2014; Maunder et al., 2014; Nekby, Rodin, & Ozcan, 2009). This emphasis is particularly important since social motivation and cultural engagement influences a person's academic achievement (Hawkes, 2014).

While acknowledging their limitations, theories of socialization and acculturation can provide insight into how students of color matriculate into and make progress through STEM doctoral programs. The recognition that students of color may have completed their undergraduate education at a HBCU or minority serving institution with a distinctly different culture than the graduate institution, or the feelings of isolation associated with being the only student of color in a graduate STEM program is necessary to fully understand the student experience via these theoretical lenses (Azizova & Felder, 2017). Both theoretical approaches are connected to issues of identity, a salient factor in academic success and adaptation at any educational level (Nekby et al., 2009). Identity works in multiple directions—that is, identity is defined not only how someone sees themselves, but also how others see that person.

When considering theories of socialization and acculturation, more attention to the anticipatory experiences of students of color in STEM fields is relevant. These experiences might include K–12 curricula, out of school learning opportunities, summer bridge programs, or the influence of completing undergraduate studies at a minority-serving institution. These experiences might result in positive and negative conclusions about pursuing a STEM career. Also, recognizing that the kind of work a student does can influence perceptions of the field shape research into the student experience as well as approaches towards practice. Perhaps the student is involved in highly collaborative research that spans multiple institutions, or even countries, or perhaps the student finds motivation in doing work with a perceived social value. These nuances emphasize the individual student identity and the relationship between identity and daily practice. Further, understanding the student's relationship with other people, including faculty and peers as well as family, friends, and neighbors, offers a more holistic understanding of how individuals can positively or negatively shape the student's perception of success. For example, understanding why a same-race mentorship is effective is as important as understanding why it is not. Exploring the layers of identity and how those are manifested and rewarded within the academic institution matter.

Conclusion. The sociocultural nature of education highlights that the student experience is highly dependent on the context, including the institutional and departmental context as well as the individuals with whom the student interacts (Hawkes, 2014). Challenges encountered by students of color in STEM graduate programs include amassing content knowledge and learning new research techniques, and span onwards to interacting with the surrounding context in a way that supports and furthers their unique identities. Providing support for these students should be an intentional and reflexive effort (Twale, Weidman, & Bethea, 2016), including consideration given to the effect that the underrepresented group's culture has on the dominant culture, both simultaneously and independently. In order to expand our understand of how students of color experience their STEM educational trajectories, understanding why and how race and ethnicity matter is crucial

REFERENCES

Amenkhienan, C. A., & Kogan, L. R. (2004). Engineering students' perceptions of academic activities and support services: Factors that influence their academic performance. *College Student Journal, 38*(4), 523–540.

Ampaw, F. D., & Jaeger, A. J. (2011). Understanding the factors affecting degree completion of doctoral women in the science and engineering fields. *New Directions for Institutional Research, 2011*(152), 59–73.

Azizova, Z. T., & Felder, P. P. (2017). Understanding racial/ethnic meaning making: Narrative analysis of STE [A] M doctoral student experiences. *Studies in Graduate and Postdoctoral Education, 8*(2), 144–168.

Chun, H., Marin, M. R., Schwartz, J. P., Pham, A., & Castro-Olivo, S. M. (2016). Psychosociocultural structural model of college success among Latina/o students in Hispanic-serving institutions. *Journal of Diversity in Higher Education, 9*(4), 385.

Council of Graduate Schools. (2010). *PhD completion and attrition: Policies and practices to promote student success.* Washington, DC: Council of Graduate Schools.

de Valero, Y. (2001). Departmental Factors Affecting Time-to-Degree and Completion Rates of Doctoral Students at One Land-Grant Research Institution. *The Journal of Higher Education, 72*(3), 341–367. doi:10.2307/2649335

Felder, P. P. (2015). Edward A. Bouchet: A model for understanding African Americans and their doctoral experience. *Journal of African American Studies, 19*(1), 3–17.

Felder, P., & Freeman, S. (2016). Exploring doctoral student socialization and the African American experience. *The Western Journal of Black Studies, 40*(2), 77–79.

Felder, P., Stevenson, H. C., & Gasman, M. (2014). Understanding race in doctoral student socialization. *International Journal of Doctoral Studies, 9*, 21–42.

Graham, E. (2013). The experiences of minority doctoral students at elite research institutions. *New Directions for Higher Education, 163*, 77–87.

Hawkes, L. (2014, March). *The development of the social and academic identities of international students in English speaking higher education institutions.* Paper presented to York St John University, School of Foundation and English Language Studies, BPP University.

Herzig, A. H. (2004). Becoming mathematics: Women and students of color choosing and leaving doctoral mathematics. *Review of Educational Research, 74*(2), 171–214.

Holley, K. A., & Caldwell, M. L. (2012). The challenges of designing and implementing a doctoral student mentoring program. *Innovative Higher Education, 37*(3), 243–253.

Hurtado, S., Clayton-Pedersen, A. R., Allen, W. R., & Milem, J. F. (1998). Enhancing campus climates for racial/ethnic diversity: Educational policy and practice. *The Review of Higher Education, 21*(3), 279–302.

Ibarra, R. A. (2001). *Beyond affirmative action: Reframing the context of higher education.* Madison, WI: University of Wisconsin Press.

Johnson, J., Jones, T., Haddad, G., Wilcox, C., & Wilcox, J. K. G. (2016). Strategies to enhance the role of HBCUs in increasing the science, technology, engineering, mathematics, and medical (STEMM) workforce. In *Setting a new agenda for student engagement and retention in Historically Black Colleges and Universities* (pp. 96–118). Hershey, PA: IGI Global.

Joseph, J. (2007). *The experiences of African American graduate students: A cultural transition* (EdD dissertation). Los Angeles, CA: University of Southern California.

Joseph, J (2013). The impact of historically black colleges and universities on doctoral students. In K. Holley & J. Joseph (Eds.), *Increasing diversity in doctoral education: Implications for theory and practice* (pp. 67–76). San Francisco, CA: Jossey-Bass.

Joseph, J. (2014). Acculturation, not socialization, for African American females in the STEM fields. *Sociological Research Online, 19*(2), 8.

Ko, L., Kachchaf, R., Hodari, A., & Ong, M. (2014). Agency of women of color in physics and astronomy: Strategies for persistence and success. *Journal of Women and Minorities in Science and Engineering, 20*(2), 171–195.

Lappe, F. M., & DuBois, P. M. (1997). Building social capital without looking backward. *National Civic Review, 14,* 20.

Maltese, A. V., & Tai, R. H. (2011). Pipeline persistence: Examining the association of educational experiences with earned degrees in STEM among US students. *Science Education, 95*(5), 877–907.

Marsh, K. (2013). "Staying Black": The demonstration of racial identity and womanhood among a group of young high-achieving Black women. *International Journal of Qualitative Studies in Education, 26*(10), 1213–1237.

Maton, K. I., Pollard, S. A., McDougall Weise, T. V., & Hrabowski, F. A. (2012). Meyerhoff Scholars Program: A strengths-based, institution-wide approach to increasing diversity in science, technology, engineering, and mathematics. *Mount Sinai Journal of Medicine: A Journal of Translational and Personalized Medicine, 79*(5), 610–623.

Maunder, R., Di Napoli, R., Borg, M., Fry, H., Walsh, E., & Jiang, X. (2014). Acculturation into UK academic practice: the experiences of international doctoral students and academic staff at two research-intensive universities. *Academic Practice, Work and Cultures, 10*(2).

Myers, C. B., & Pavel, D. M. (2011). Underrepresented students in STEM: The transition from undergraduate to graduate programs. *Journal of Diversity in Higher Education, 4*(2), 90.

National Center for Education Statistics. (2013). *Digest of Education Statistics.* Institute of Education Sciences, U. S. Department of Education, Washington, DC.

National Science Foundation. (2014). Retrieved from https://www.nsf.gov/statistics/seind14/

National Science Foundation. (2018). *Science and engineering indicators.* https://www.nsf.gov/statistics/2018/nsb20181/

Nekby, L., Rodin, M., & Ozcan, G. (2009). Acculturation identity and higher education: Is there a trade-off between ethnic identity and education? *International Migration Review, 43*(4), 938–973.

Ong, M., Wright, C., Espinosa, L., & Orfield, G. (2011). Inside the double bind: A synthesis of empirical research on undergraduate and graduate women of color in science, technology, engineering, and mathematics. *Harvard Educational Review, 81*(2), 172–209.

Ong, M., Smith, J. M., & Ko, L. T. (2018). Counterspaces for women of color in STEM higher education: Marginal and central spaces for persistence and success. *Journal of Research in Science Teaching, 55*(2), 206–245.

Phinney, J., Horenczyk, G., Liebkind, K., & Vedder, P. (2001). Ethnic identity, immigration, and well-being: An interactional perspective. *Journal of Social Issues,* 57(3), 493–510.

Settles, I. (2006). Use of an intersectional framework to understand Black women's racial and gender identities. *Sex Roles, 54,* 13.

Strayhorn, T. L. (2015). Factors influencing Black males' preparation for college and success in STEM majors: A mixed methods study. *Western Journal of Black Studies, 39*(1), 45.

Thoman, D. B., Muragishi, G. A., & Smith, J. L. (2017). Research microcultures as socialization contexts for underrepresented science students. *Psychological Science, 28*(6), 760–773.

Twale, D., Weidman, J. C., & Bethea, K. (2016). Conceptualizing socialization of graduate students of color: Revisiting the Weidman-Twale-Stein Framework. *The Western Journal of Black Studies, 40*(2), 15.

Weidman, J. C., Twale, D. J., & Stein, E. L. (2001). *Socialization of graduate and professional students in higher education: A perilous passage?* San Francisco, CA: Jossey-Bass.

CHAPTER 2

STRATEGIES FOR USING CRITICAL SYSTEMS THEORY TO SUPPORT SOCIALIZATION OF UNDERGRADUATE AFRICAN AMERICAN STUDENTS IN STEM

Sonyia C. Richardson and Lenora Crabtree
University of North Carolina

On the first day of class, the professor stands at the front of a large lecture hall and issues a dire warning. "Look to your left and right at the persons sitting on either side of you. One of you will not be here at the end of the semester." This story, often told by those who have experienced an introductory STEM course, provides a graphic depiction of the general features of STEM culture at many universities. Research indicates that the majority of students who leave STEM majors do so in the first two years of undergraduate education when much of their exposure to STEM culture occurs in introductory courses (Gasiewski, Eagan, Garcia, Hurtado, & Chang, 2012). Consequently, these courses have a significant impact on student socialization and persistence in STEM, and subsequent completion of a STEM degree.

Seeing The HiddEn Minority, pp. 17–36
Copyright © 2020 by Information Age Publishing
All rights of reproduction in any form reserved.

18 • S. C. RICHARDSON and L. CRABTREE

Supporting the socialization of students within science, technology, engineering, and math (STEM) majors is a pathway towards ensuring interest, persistence and completion of these degree programs (Eddy & Brownell, 2016; Kozan et al., 2017). Socialization is defined as "the process by which persons acquire the knowledge, skills, and dispositions that make them more or less effective members of their society" (Brim, 1966, p. 3). While STEM disciplines have primarily catered to a White male group culture (Eisenhart & Finkel, 1998; Johnson, 2001), the current focus on increasing diversity to accelerate and add value to the field warrant different approaches for the inclusion of diverse students. Students from groups underrepresented in STEM (African American, Latinx, and Native American) enroll in colleges and universities with an intent to major in a STEM field at the same rate as White students but do not obtain STEM degrees at the same rate (Hurtado, Newman, Tran & Chang, 2010). One contributing factor involves limited socialization of African American students within STEM culture. A focus on socialization, however, should not place the onus on African American undergraduate students or encourage them to acculturate to a predominantly White STEM culture. On the contrary, socialization for African American undergraduate students within STEM disciplines requires a focus on emancipation and social justice within systems to reject dominant ideologies while encouraging the use of individual supports and resources. Thus, we propose an approach to socialization that encourages African American students to achieve success not through conforming to the dominant STEM culture but by being agents of its transformation.

CRITICAL SYSTEMS THEORY OVERVIEW (SONYIA)

Ludwig von Bertlalanffy (1968) is acknowledged as the founder of general systems theory which focuses on the overall function of a system by examining subentities within the system that exude interdependent influence on an identified subject or structure. General systems theory investigates bidirectional influences within systems and how they contribute to the functioning of the whole system or the individual. Incidences occurring within one system have an impact on the other systems.

Researchers have incorporated general systems theory within the sciences as a means of shifting to an integrated approach whereby concepts are interconnected and related (Gulyaev & Stonyer, 2002). Examination of interactions among four major domains and the resulting systemic change due to the interactions was further examined through ecological systems theory (Bronfenbrenner, 1977). These systems operate within four identified domains including the microsystem, mesosystem, exosystem, and macrosystem that are centered around an identified or defined individual

Strategies for Using Critical Systems Theory   19

or entity. We will utilize an undergraduate African American student in a STEM field to explain application to each of these systems. This identified subject is not further defined based on gender, socioeconomic factors, or geographic location, although we do acknowledge that there may differences based on these features.

The microsystem includes individuals or entities that interact daily with the student or provide regular support. The student's microsystem may include professors, peers, and family members. The mesosystem involves group based or collective entities that interact with the student on a regular basis. This includes the curriculum and pedagogy employed by instructors, cohorts of students, and interaction that occurs within research laboratories. The exosystem includes environmental factors that have an impact but are not directly engaged with the student on a consistent basis. Examples include departmental and university policies and the university community. Societal factors and existing ideologies, attitudes and behaviors towards the subject comprise the macrosystem which may include factors that impact the student's preparation for STEM coursework as well as stereotypes or beliefs about African American students.

Understanding systemic level change that occurs as a result of interaction between domains provides additional insight into how parts impact the whole. When considering the needs of students of color existing in systems that are designed and maintained by and for the dominant culture, it is essential to examine systems through a critical lens. "Critical systems theory (CST) brings a system thinking lens to help educational researchers understand the complex nature of educational systems and problems" (Watson & Watson, 2011, p. 64). CST incorporates themes of critique, pluralism, emancipation, and social justice within a systemic perspective allowing for a fuller understanding of system interaction (Schecter, 1991; Flood & Jackson, 1991). Pluralism supports the acceptance of multiple methodological approaches grounded in theory (Watson & Watson, 2011). It accepts that there is not a singular element or method but a combination of elements that impact the system. Emancipation involves "freeing of the system and systems individuals from any kind oppression that disables them to critique and fully develop their potential" (Watson & Watson, 2011, p. 116). Social justice encourages action and advocacy, addressing oppressive structures and systems to increase access and opportunity.

In alignment with CST, we argue for the integration of critique, pluralism, emancipation, and social justice within a systems framework focusing on solutions for socialization of African American undergraduate students in STEM. African American undergraduate students in STEM are the subjects for this systems level perspective. First, we present a framework for application of CST to socialization of African American undergraduate students in STEM. Next, we review literature related to socialization and

20 S. C. RICHARDSON and L. CRABTREE

STEM culture using a systems level lens. Lastly, we propose solutions for support of the socialization of African American undergraduate students within each system level.

FRAMEWORK FOR SOCIALIZATION OF AFRICAN AMERICAN UNDERGRADUATE STUDENTS IN STEM

The socialization of African American undergraduate students in STEM through a critical systems theory approach is visually depicted in Figure 2.1. African American undergraduate students in STEM serve as the subjects in the system. The main themes of CST including critique, pluralism, social justice, and emancipation feed directly into the system and have bidirectional influence, illustrating the necessity for critique of the system and recognition of variables that potentially oppress students. When it is discovered that a factor within the system is causing strain on the system, it is important to uncover it and free students from the stressor's negative impact.

The four systems supporting African American students through socialization in STEM are listed in the circles. We understand that not every student will have support of each variable listed at each system level. However, this is a general overview of the supports available to most students.

We suggest that positive interaction between the systems and CST principles can result in successful socialization of African American students in STEM leading to the acquisition of knowledge, skills, and behaviors necessary for persistence and completion of a STEM degree. As students acquire these skills, knowledge, and behavior, their success flows back into the system and impacts other students. Understanding each of these systems, their impact, and interactions between systems provides a comprehensive perspective on the socialization of African American undergraduate students in STEM. Additionally, we argue that full inclusion of African American students in STEM requires acceptance and acknowledgement of this systems level approach that is supporting students through persistence in the degree. To approach these students through common individualistic, competitive, and White domination ideals, does not support their engagement or desire to persist in the STEM field.

STEM CULTURE AT THE SYSTEMS LEVEL

Microsystem Supports

Professors. In traditional STEM introductory courses, the professor standing at the front of a large lecture hall is the exalted bearer of knowledge.

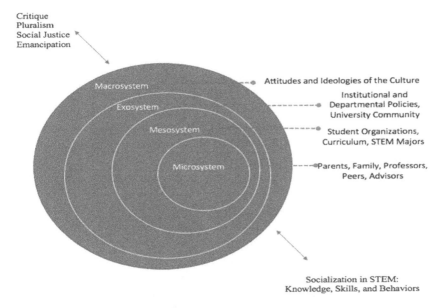

Figure 2.1. Strategies for utlizing critical theory to support socialization of undergraduate Afican American students.

Information is transmitted in a unidirectional manner, as opposed to being co-constructed by a group of learners including the teacher (Wood, 2009). At large, predominantly White research institutions, professors in STEM courses often perceive themselves to be first and foremost scientists; teaching is a secondary task (Anderson et al., 2011). Students who experience marginalization in the STEM culture may feel that their instructors maintain their distance and purposely weed out students (Eastman, Chrisman, Zion, & Yerrick, 2017; Johnson, 2007; Lindemann, Britton, & Zundl, 2016). In large lecture halls, the professor's standard end of class query, "Any questions?" is unlikely to elicit responses from African American students who see few students in the room who look like them and have been socialized to avoid standing out in threatening situations (Johnson, 2007). For students who experienced success in STEM coursework in high school through warm, supportive relationships with teachers, the transition is especially challenging (Eastman et al., 2017; Johnson, 2007). Lacking meaningful interactions with professors, African American students may develop a reluctance to seek assistance with difficult course material, a disposition counter-productive to their persistence and success in STEM.

Peers. In this challenging environment, peer support should play an important role. Instead, an atmosphere of individualism, exclusivity and competition pervades introductory courses in STEM at many universities (Garibay, 2015; Gasiewski et al., 2012; Stephens, Fryberg, Markus, Johnson, & Covarrubias, 2012). Warned from the first day of class that one third of students will be gone by December, potential colleagues become competitors in a dogged game of survival (Gasiewski et al., 2012), an environment in sharp contrast to the collectivist community in which many students underrepresented in STEM have been socialized (Estrada et al., 2016). Large class sizes create an intimidating atmosphere that impedes student interaction and collegiality (Johnson, 2007). African American students may choose to abandon a STEM major instead of adjusting to the dominant culture that promotes isolation and self-achievement (Puritty et al., 2017) and values the success of the individual as opposed to the collective group (Estrada et al., 2016).

In contrast to the competitive atmosphere of many PWIs students planning to major in STEM fields at two historically Black colleges (HBCUs) are socialized to draw upon their peers for encouragement and support. From the moment students arrive on the Spelman campus, they are encouraged to view their peers as supportive members of the same team, or family (Perna et al., 2009). A similar culture is encouraged at Morehouse through the Peer Led Team Learning (PLTL) initiative, a program that creates an atmosphere in which peers are viewed "as a source of support; everyone wants each person to succeed" (Gasman, Nguyen, Conrad, Lundberg, & Commodore, 2017, p. 189). Faculty members recruit and train PLTL leaders from among previous students who struggled in introductory courses. In weekly meetings, PLTL leaders encourage team members to share concepts with which they are struggling and work together until everyone has achieved a greater level of understanding. According to Gasman et al. (2017), "because the PLTL leader is selected by his struggles to achieve ... he is capable of helping his peers work out challenging problems, as well as socializing them to be in their best state of learning" (p. 196).

Parents. While parents/guardians often play a vital role in providing support to their undergraduate students, literature is scant regarding their involvement or contributions to assisting with socialization and persistence in STEM disciplines. Ing (2013) found a positive relationship between persistence in STEM careers and parental motivational factors. These factors contributed to students persisting through STEM careers but the study was not specific to cultural factors or socialization within the STEM discipline. Alternatively, Maton and Hrabowski (2004) found that while parental influence was an important factor for African American student persistence in STEM, parental characteristics were also influencing factors. This includes the educational level of the parents, income level, and residential community the parents reside in. Accordingly, these factors may also have an impact on socialization of students in STEM.

Mesosystem Supports

Curriculum. Traditionally, knowledge acquisition in STEM involves students learning discipline specific facts and concepts that explain natural phenomena. Faced with a monumental amount of information to convey in introductory courses, instructors may fail to connect facts and concepts with issues of concern to society. Traditional STEM curriculum that fails to take into account the development of students' social responsibility (Garibay, 2015) may dampen students' perceptions of their capacity to address the needs of marginalized communities through a career in STEM. This disconnect between acquiring knowledge and doing work that brings about social justice alienates young scientists and discourages some students from pursuing scientific careers (Garibay, 2015; Puritty et al., 2017) Numerous studies confirm the negative impact this omission has on engagement and persistence for students from marginalized groups, including African American students in STEM (Campbell et al., 2014; Hurtado et al., 2010; Johnson, 2007; Thoman, Brown, Mason, Harmsen, & Smith, 2015).

Pedagogy. Acquisition of the knowledge and skills required to succeed is an important aspect of the socialization process. Studies conducted over a 30-year period support the assertion that collaborative, active learning increases student learning in STEM (Fairweather, 2008; Haak, HilleRisLambers, Pitre, & Freeman, 2011; Tsui, 2007: Wood, 2009). Compared with Supplemental Instruction (SI) programs that are time and personnel intensive, changes in course structure are a more cost-effective way to raise the performance of all students, especially those who may have had limited opportunities for advanced STEM coursework prior to college (Haak et al., 2011). Current research indicates that increasing the degree of structure within a course and providing opportunities for collaboration during classes has a positive impact on course performance by African American and first-generation college students (Eddy & Hogan, 2014). Surveys conducted in traditional lecture-based introductory Biology courses taught at one large PWI found that African American students were less likely to verbally participate in class than students of other ethnicities (Eddy & Hogan, 2017). In post-course surveys of transformed STEM classes, African American students were more likely to participate verbally in a class with the described interventions than in a traditional lecture setting, an outcome researchers attribute to the increased sense of community in transformed courses (Eddy & Hogan, 2017).

Research Experiences. Engaging in science research contributes significantly to a students' assimilation into STEM culture and positively impacts persistence in STEM majors. Analysis of data from a longitudinal, cross-institutional survey of over 3,000 undergraduate students revealed that students from groups underrepresented in STEM who participated in undergraduate research programs "increased their chances of obtaining or continuing to progress toward completing a STEM degree, by an impressive 17.4 percentage points" (Chang, Sharkness, Hurtado & Newman, 2014). Participation in undergraduate research also increases students' career aspirations in STEM and their interest in pursuing graduate work following graduation (Carpi, Ronan, Falconer, & Lents, 2017).

A number of potential barriers to participation in research experiences have been identified. These include a lack of STEM social capital (awareness of research opportunities, their importance and how to obtain them), financial capital (an inability to spend significant hours volunteering in a lab or travel to another state for a funded research opportunity) and unconscious bias on the part of faculty regarding which students are best suited for research (Bangera & Brownell, 2014). For students who surmount barriers and work in a laboratory under the mentorship of a research professor, the disconnect between conducting laboratory research and altruistic goals may negatively influence their desire to pursue a career in STEM (Thoman et al., 2015). Undergraduate and graduate students representing groups underrepresented in STEM participated in focus groups during which investigators asked how their research experience could be improved. Collectively, students expressed a desire that STEM training be adapted to "include or make room for a social justice component" (Campbell et al., 2014, p. 589).

Exosystem Supports

Institutional and Departmental Policies. Within the exosystem, institutional and departmental policies play a significant role in socialization of undergraduate African American students. Killpack and Melón (2016) suggest that policy changes have resulted from recognition of a demographic gap in the STEM field thus increasing access for students of color. Policies that embrace and reinforce dominant values may perpetuate the underrepresentation and exclusion of African American students in STEM. For example, rigid admission policies that are meant to identify students who may be successful with completion of STEM degrees, can weed out or exclude students who have potential to be successful in STEM but have not had access to the same resources. As a result, underrepresentation of African American students in STEM

Strategies for Using Critical Systems Theory   25

affords limited opportunities for diverse students to exist in spaces with students who share similar lived experiences.

In a startlingly honest and introspective study, engineering faculty at a large, predominantly White STEM-focused university conducted an analysis of a program designed to increase graduation of students from underrepresented groups in STEM by increasing enrollment and support (full tuition, a summer bridge program, advising and social support) for high-performing students from the local urban school system (Eastman et al., 2017). Data revealed that despite an overall retention rate of 85%, attrition from STEM majors by students in the program mirrored national averages. Through interviews with students, professors and administrators the authors uncovered policies that promote a dominant White ethos of meritocracy, privilege and power and ignore the specific educational needs of students. According to the authors,

> University administration believe they are doing the right thing to help underrepresented students, but in reality, they are only providing a means to "mold" the students to fit the environment that excluded them in the first place.... As long as science and engineering continue to be taught with only the knowledge and ways of knowing of White men counting, no amount of scaffolding from support programs will provide equity for the students they serve. (Eastman et al., 2017, p. 902)

Macrosystem

Access and Equity in K–12 Education. Socialization of undergraduate African American students in STEM courses begins prior their acceptance into a university. One study of factors influencing college completion revealed that academic coursework at the high school level accounted for a greater portion of the variation between African American and White students than any other factor including socioeconomic status (Flores, Park, & Baker, 2017). Opportunities for African American students to participate in advanced coursework while in high school are limited due to under-referrals from teachers and counselors, lack of access to Gifted Education programs and low numbers of Advanced Placement (AP) courses offered at schools with high numbers of African American students (Darity & Jolla, 2009; Milner & Ford, 2007; Whiting & Ford, 2009). According to one study of schools with an African American-White AP enrollment gaps, 69% of African American students whose PSAT scores indicated potential for success in AP courses were not enrolled in those courses (Theokas & Saaris, 2013). As a result, many African American students do not experience socialization into rigorous and demanding college level courses during high school and may not have the same level of knowledge or skills to navigate challenging courses at the postsecondary level (Eastman et al., 2017; Perna et al., 2009).

Societal Attitudes and Ideologies. Several recently released works of literature and film emphasize the contributions of African Americans in STEM fields (Shetterly, 2016). These depictions, however, are rare, and media portrayals of African Americans are more commonly negative. Educational programs echo this deficit framework by focusing on how to "fix" African American students instead of emphasizing how the strengths of successful scholars have been developed and nurtured (Maton & Hbrowski, 2004). In addition, the language surrounding efforts to increase recruitment and retention of African American students in STEM is problematic. Academic publications, government and foundation reports frequently refer to the importance of developing and maintaining a diverse STEM workforce to ensure that the U.S. economy remains globally competitive (Eastman et al., 2017; National Science Foundation [NSF], 2015, 2018). This emphasis on a need for workers to maintain American competitiveness is eerily reminiscent of the roles African Americans were forced to play in the U.S. economy of previous centuries. Research and innovation in STEM fields requires thinkers and problem solvers, not workers, to address global challenges. Through the incorporation of a critical perspective that highlights emancipation, pluralism and social justice, students can be encouraged to surmount the inevitable challenges that occur as they prepare to make their own unique contributions to this vital endeavor.

STRATEGIES FOR SUPPORTING SOCIALIZATION OF AFRICAN AMERICAN STUDENTS IN STEM

Specific strategies for supporting African American Undergraduate students with socialization in STEM disciplines are provided through a critical systems framework. Discussion of strategies at the microsystem, mesosystem, exosystem, and macrosystem levels is provided to aid understanding of factors and entities that assist with socialization. A critical analysis provides a deeper understanding of how systems may be navigated to provide optimum support.

Microsystem Supports

College Professors. College professors within a variety of disciplines are included within the microsystem as they have the opportunity to provide support and direction for students. It is important for African

American undergraduate students to form connections with professors with whom they can relate, individuals who may have shared lived experiences, research agendas of interest or demeanors that feel supportive to the student. Professors within STEM disciplines are encouraged to create classroom environments that support diverse learners by adopting a pedagogical approach that centers the learner and encourages student agency. Open classroom environments in which professors are receptive to student questions, encourage dialogue, and provide additional instructional opportunities outside of the classroom are more likely to have engage students who may be marginalized in STEM (Gasiewski et al., 2012).

Strategies for instructors to assist with teaching diverse student learners include: (1) Increase course structure to scaffold learning for students (Eddy & Hogan, 2014; Haak et al., 2011); (2) Provide opportunities for students to collaborate during class through active learning exercises (Fairweather, 2008; Haak et al., 2011; Tsui, 2007: Wood, 2009); (3) Train SI leaders to ask questions and engage students in problem solving as opposed to conducting lectures (Gasman, Nguyen, Conrad, Lundberg, & Commodore, 2017); (4) Encourage students who do not demonstrate high levels of proficiency to utilize SI sessions or ask for individual help; (5) Do not assume that all students are aware of college level classroom norms and behaviors including attendance and the use of computers, cell phones, netiquette; (6) Allow students to make suggestions regarding additional rules and classroom norms.

Peers. Peer groups play an integral role in providing support to undergraduate African American students. Undergraduate students in STEM courses should be encouraged to view each other as colleagues, not competitors. Research science, health occupations, engineering and computer science are inherently cooperative fields in which teams of individuals work together toward common goals. Socializing students in a competitive culture through undergraduate STEM courses promotes a false view of science and discourages African American students from persisting in STEM majors. Harper (2007) found that African American male high achieving students attribute much of their collegiate success to same race peer groups who they reported playing a significant role. Students are encouraged to seek out or create African American preprofessional, STEM-focused and non-STEM-focused organizations on campus to support their personal and professional goals.

Small group interactions among students can begin in class (Eddy & Hogan, 2014). Students can be encouraged to discuss a previously posted problem, case study or relevant societal issue with persons sitting near them. By encouraging interaction within the classroom, faculty members assist students who may not know others in the class to develop the nucleus of a support system. Structured study groups that meet outside of class and foster a sense of community benefit African American students (Tsui, 2007). Following the Morehouse model (Gasman et al., 2017), small groups leaders should be chosen whose own background and experience as a struggling, but now successful, student equips them to mentor others effectively. Near-peer tutoring sessions should allow students to discuss challenging material and discover problem solving strategies collectively.

Parents or Legal Guardians. Parents or legal guardians with an understanding or experience within the STEM field have a greater influence on student aspirations in STEM (Holmes, Gore, Smith, & Lloyd, 2018). Parents with experience within STEM should utilize this social capital to support their child with socialization and persistence in the STEM field. Parents with limited experience in STEM can also play an important role by connecting their child with a mentor in the STEM field and maintaining open communication regarding STEM. When identifying a potential STEM mentor, parents should consider individuals who already exist within the child's network such as teachers, neighbors, and church members. Parents should encourage their child to shadow the mentor at work and learn more about their academic preparation. Lastly, the mentor should be someone with whom the student can relate. Mentors serve important roles such as mediators for students but are often not sought for students who excel academically (Ogbu, 2004). Even when a child is excelling in the STEM field, parents should still seek mentorship.

Mesosystem

Curriculum and Pedagogy. Curricular and pedagogical choices by faculty play significant roles in the acculturation of students in STEM. Among STEM scholars, knowledge of culturally relevant pedagogies and critical race theory are rare (Eastman et al., 2017). Consequently, university-level STEM education reinforces socioeconomic and educational inequities rooted in communities and K–12 education systems through a failure at the institutional level to reimagine STEM culture from a holistic perspective. Critical pedagogies that challenge faculty to consider the value of constructivist learning and confront how lecture-based instruction maintains power and privilege are needed (Eastman et al., 2017).

Inequities in the distribution of resources including healthy food, clean water, and healthcare are critical issues facing society in the 21st century. These challenges require solutions that can be developed through STEM research and innovation, however, they are rarely discussed in introductory STEM courses. Equipped with the knowledge that students from marginalized groups are motivated by issues that impact their communities, faculty should adapt curriculum to emphasize relevant topics during lectures and discussions (Garibay, 2015). Providing time during class for utility-value exercises, short writing assignments in which students make explicit connections between course material and issues of personal relevance, has also been found to improve student engagement and increase learning (Harackiewicz, Canning, Tibbetts, Priniski, & Hyde, 2016).

Research Experiences. The process of acquiring skills and dispositions are essential aspects of socialization in STEM. Working in a research lab provides an important introduction to the methods and tools of a specific STEM discipline. Undergraduate research experiences also allow individuals to develop the mental framework essential for success in a STEM field. The NSF funds stipend-supported summer Research Experiences for Undergraduates (REUs) at universities across the United States. Students should work with advisors to explore opportunities to conduct research as soon as possible during their undergraduate years.

Adjusting to the unique culture of a research laboratory is not an easy process. Each lab is different and students may feel out of place in this unusual setting. Scientific research is an iterative process; experiments rarely work the first time and failures in the laboratory are common. The challenging laboratory environment, coupled with marginalization, may cause students to feel as if a STEM career is not the best choice for them. Support from caring professors, advisors, peers, and family is essential at this juncture.

Providing opportunities for undergraduate research scientists to share their findings with the public is a powerful way to encourage student agency and enhance a collectivist orientation in STEM. As students conduct research they should be encouraged to investigate ways that new scientific knowledge may have a positive impact on society. Learning to translate complex ideas for nonscience audiences is valuable training and leads to increased research productivity as investigators are challenged to think differently about their own work and opportunities to broaden participation in science expand (Heath et al., 2014; Jensen, Rouquier, Kreimer, & Croissant, 2008). Students involved in undergraduate research who are from the local community can play a vital role connecting research scientists with science educators in nearby schools. As student researchers conduct outreach in K–12 classrooms they become valuable role models, transforming perceptions about "who" does science as they share their new knowledge.

Exosystem Supports

Institutional and Departmental Policies. Departments and academic units are encouraged to review existing policies, including those related to admission and matriculation, to determine if they are "weeding out" students of color or preventing their successful progression. The development of policies that support the progression of diverse students, while providing necessary supports and infrastructure, will aid in their retention within these disciplines thus emancipating them from rigid rules and norms.

Programs are also encouraged to identify how their departmental policies and structures or encouraging reforms in teaching among its faculty members. Departments are the primary drivers for changes in instructional styles, pedagogical approaches, and quality teaching among faculty (Shadle, Marker, & Earl, 2017). While professors may utilize student evaluations and self-appraisal as a means to improve their teacher, sustained changes across the department should rely more heavily on departmental level change (Shadle et al., 2017).

Equitable Access Within Departments. Alongside reform of instructional strategies and pedagogical approaches, is the importance of ensuring that there is equitable access within the department. "Policies and practices that ensure equitable access to the best STEM teaching and learning are not widespread" (U.S. Department of Education, 2016, p. 2). Inconsistencies have been noted across universities. Policies should ensure access and inclusion in program admission, rigorous course offerings, research and work study opportunities, scholarships, grants and awards. Departments are charged with ensuring that students have access to opportunities that may not be available to all students, particularly brown and black faces, through policies that focus on diversity and inclusiveness as priorities. It is important to maintain data on representation within the department, particularly with regards to research and lab opportunities. Department level data may be able to identify where there is overrepresentation of certain gender and races.

Positive Socialization at HBCUs. Analysis of the STEM culture at highly selective historically Black colleges and universities (HBCUs), points the way toward socialization practices that not only support African American students in STEM but have the potential to transform STEM culture in a way that is beneficial to all. At Morehouse, an all-male HBCU, administrators purposely recruit faculty who are committed to mentoring as well as research, "teacher scholars" and "leaders in active learning" who "guide students into college and STEM programs and come alongside them as research partners" (Gasman et al., 2017, p. 192). According to Gasman et al. (2017), the STEM faculty at Morehouse is "committed to fostering relationships that break down barriers to success" thus embracing a philosophy that all students can succeed (p. 193). Consequently, students describe their professors as valuable guides and motivators. Interactions between students and professors in STEM classrooms at Morehouse resemble a conversational approach to learning as opposed to a traditional lecture.

Students at Spelman College, an all-female HBCU, describe the environment in STEM as one that sets them up to succeed (Perna et al., 2009). Professors are cognizant of the different levels of preparation that students may have received at in high school and adjust instruction to assist students in making the transition to the college STEM culture. Faculty at Spelman "have reconceptualized introductory STEM courses to serve not as mechanisms to 'weed-out' poorly performing students ... but as 'gateways' to more advanced STEM coursework" (Perna et al., 2009, p. 13). These transformative institutions provide models of how to support the socialization of African American students by adjusting the STEM culture to accommodate the needs of students as opposed to an expectation that students will acculturate to an existing culture.

Predominantly White Institutions. Students attending predominantly White institutions may benefit by seeking support from African American faculty caucus or groups. For example, the African and African American Faculty & Staff Caucus at the University of North Carolina at Charlotte provides Mentoring Circles, a mentoring program to students of color across the university. As a result of the decreased representation of African American faculty members within STEM areas, the caucus developed this initiative to connect students with African American faculty members across the campus. Additionally, the group travels the campus for mentoring initiatives and intentionally targets STEM areas for meetings. Through a partnership with African American faculty in the College of Engineering, the Mentoring Circles program held a program in the College of Engineering which brought approximately 25 African American faculty and staff members to the engineering building to provide direct mentoring and support and establish connections with students of color. These initiatives have been critical for ensuring students have an opportunity to connect with diverse faculty.

Macrosystem Strategies

Access and Equity in K–12 Education. It is imperative that educational systems advocate for access and equity to AP, honors, and college level courses for K–12 students. Increasing access to advanced courses for diverse youth will enhance their preparation for undergraduate and graduate work in STEM fields. Opportunities to enroll in and complete challenging courses provides socialization in the required work and study habits necessary for success at the collegiate level. Advocacy for access to these courses should begin at the elementary level with a focus on increased identification for gifted education programs. Inclusion of diverse youth in elementary and middle school gifted education programs creates a pipeline for access to more rigorous courses and content in high school.

Advocacy must extend beyond simply increasing access and inclusion to gifted education and advanced course content and should extend to educational policy definitions and guidelines. For example, exclusionary policies that rely solely on standardized test scores for admittance into gifted education programs and advanced courses further perpetuates limited access for diverse youth. Policy reform must occur in order for sustained and prolonged impact to occur.

Societal Attitudes and Ideologies. The cultural narrative surrounding recruitment and retention of African American students in STEM should also be addressed. An intentional focus on past and present contributions of African Americans in STEM disciplines can create a vital counter-narrative to deficit frameworks. This new emphasis should highlight the ways in which African American scientists have and will advance STEM fields through scholarship, research and innovation as opposed to focusing on employment and "workforce" initiatives. The challenges of the 21st century and beyond require innovators who are able to think outside of a Western, Eurocentric box and imagine new solutions to the world's most pressing problems. A critical approach to STEM education supports pluralism and emancipation at the system level, encouraging the involvement of students whose varied ways of knowing and doing will provide solutions to society's most vexing problems and answers to questions not yet asked.

CONCLUSION

Imagine a classroom in which the professor walks among students grouped at tables or stands in the aisle of a lecture hall and states,

> Look to your right and to your left. The students sitting on either side of you are your colleagues, your teammates, your family members in this course. All of you will be here in December if you will work together to be successful. Now, introduce yourself to your each other and let's get started.

The success of students in STEM majors requires an understanding of socialization factors that impact the overall adjustment, retention, and persistence in these fields. Utilizing CST, we have provided a framework to guide understanding of strategies to support the socialization of African American undergraduates in STEM. It is our belief that STEM culture must be transformed to be more inclusive and meet the needs of diverse students. Our focus on socialization factors affirms existing systems and resources that can support students in STEM. This list of resources is not exhaustive and will vary according to the cultural identity and background of the student. It is our goal that this model will encourage leaders and scholars in STEM education to be receptive to the socialization of students who present with unique and diverse backgrounds.

REFERENCES

Anderson, W. A., Banerjee, U., Drennan, C. L., Elgin, S. C. R., Epstein, I. R., Handelsman, J., ... Strobel, S. A. (2011). Changing the culture of science education at research universities. *Science*, *331*(6014), 152–153.

Bangera, G., & Brownell, S. E. (2014). Course-based undergraduate research experiences can make scientific research more inclusive. *CBE—Life Sciences Education*, *13*(4), 602–606.

Brim, O. G., Jr. (1966). Socialization through the life cycle. In O. G. Brim, Jr., & S. Wheeler (Eds.), *Socialization after childhood: Two essays* (pp. 1–49). New York, NY: John Wiley.

Bronfenbrenner, U. (1977). Toward an experimental ecology of human development. *American Psychologist*, *32*(7), 513.

Campbell, A. G., Skvirsky, R., Wortis, H., Thomas, S., Kawachi, I., & Hohmann, C. (2014). NEST 2014: Views from the trainees—Talking about what matters in efforts to diversify the STEM workforce. *CBE-Life Sciences Education*, *13*(4), 587–592.

Carpi, A., Ronan, D. M., Falconer, H. M., & Lents, N. H. (2017). Cultivating minority scientists: Undergraduate research increases self-efficacy and career ambitions for underrepresented students in STEM. *Journal of Research in Science Teaching*, *54*(2), 169–194.

Chang, M. J., Sharkness, J., Hurtado, S., & Newman, C. B. (2014). What matters in college for retaining aspiring scientists and engineers from underrepresented racial groups. *Journal of Research in Science Teaching*, *51*(5), 555–580.

Darity, W., Jr., & Jolla, A. (2009). Desegregated schools with segregated education. In C. Hartman & G. Squires (Eds.),*The integration debate: Futures for American Cities* (pp. 99–117). New York, NY: Routledge.

Eastman, M. G., Christman, J., Zion, G. H., & Yerrick, R. (2017). To educate engineers or to engineer educators?: Exploring access to engineering careers. *Journal of Research in Science Teaching*, *54*(7), 884–913.

Eddy, S. L., & Brownell, S. E. (2016). Beneath the numbers: A review of gender disparities in undergraduate education across science, technology, engineering, and math disciplines. *Physical Review Physics Education Research*, *12*(2), 1–20.

Eddy, S. L., & Hogan, K. A. (2014). Getting under the hood: how and for whom does increasing course structure work? *CBE—Life Sciences Education*, *13*(3), 453–468.

Eisenhart, M., & Finkel, E. (1998). *Women's science: Learning and succeeding from the margins*. Chicago, IL: University of Chicago Press.

34 S. C. RICHARDSON and L. CRABTREE

Estrada, M., Burnett, M., Campbell, A. G., Campbell, P. B., Denetclaw, W. F., Gutiérrez, C. G., ... & Okpodu, C. M. (2016). Improving underrepresented minority student persistence in STEM. *CBE—Life Sciences Education, 15*(3), es5.

Fairweather, J. (2008). Linking evidence and promising practices in science, technology, engineering, and mathematics (STEM) undergraduate education. Board of Science Education, National Research Council, The National Academies, Washington, DC. Retrieved from https://www.nsf.gov/attachments/117803/public/Xc--Linking_Evidence--Fairweather.pdf

Flood, R. L., & Jackson, M. C. (Eds.). (1991). *Critical systems thinking: Directed readings.* New York, NY: Wiley.

Flores, S. M., Park, T. J., & Baker, D. J. (2017). The racial college completion gap: Evidence from Texas. *The Journal of Higher Education, 88*(6), 894–921.

Garibay, J. C. (2015). STEM students' social agency and views on working for social change: Are STEM disciplines developing socially and civically responsible students? *Journal of Research in Science Teaching, 52*(5), 610–632.

Gasiewski, J. A., Eagan, M. K., Garcia, G. A., Hurtado, S., & Chang, M. J. (2012). From gatekeeping to engagement: A multicontextual, mixed method study of student academic engagement in introductory STEM courses. *Research in Higher Education, 53*, 229–261.

Gasman, M., Nguyen, T., Conrad, C., Lundberg, T., & Commodore, F. (2017). Black male success in STEM: A case study of Morehouse College. *Journal of Diversity in Higher Education, 10*(2), 181–200.

Gulyaev, S. A. & Stonyer, H. R. (2002). Making a map of science: General systems theory as a conceptual framework for tertiary science education. *International Journal of Science Education, 24*(7), 753–769.

Haak, D. C., HilleRisLambers, J., Pitre, E., & Freeman, S. (2011). Increased structure and active learning reduce the achievement gap in introductory biology. *Science, 332*(6034), 1213–1216.

Harackiewicz, J. M., Canning, E. A., Tibbetts, Y., Priniski, S. J., & Hyde, J. S. (2016). Closing achievement gaps with a utility-value intervention: Disentangling race and social class. *Journal of Personality and Social Psychology, 111*(5), 745.

Harper, S. R. (2007). Peer Support for African American male college achievement: Beyond internalized racism and the burden of "acting White." *The Journal of Men's Studies, 14*(3), 337–358.

Heath, K. D., Bagley, E., Berkey, A. J., Birlenbach, D. M., Carr-Markell, M. K., Crawford, J. W., & Wesseln, C. J. (2014). Amplify the signal: Graduate training in broader impacts of scientific research. *BioScience, 64*(6), 517–523.

Holmes, K., Gore, J., Smith, M., & Lloyd, A. (2018). An integrated analysis of school students' aspirations for STEM careers: Which student and school factors are most predictive. *International Journal of Science and Mathematics Education, 16*(4), 655–675.

Hurtado, S., Newman, C. B., Tran, M. C., & Chang, M. J. (2010). Improving the rate of success for underrepresented racial minorities in STEM fields: Insights from a national project. *New Directions for Institutional Research, 148*, 5–15.

Ing, M. (2013). Can parents influence children's mathematics achievement and persistence in STEM careers. *Journal of Career Development, 41*(2), 87–103.

Jensen, P., Rouquier, J. B., Kreimer, P., & Croissant, Y. (2008). Scientists who engage with society perform better academically. *Science & Public Policy, 35*(7), 527–541.

Johnson, A. C. (2001). *Women, race and science: The academic experiences of twenty women of color with a passion for science.* University of Colorado, Boulder, CO.

Johnson, A. C. (2007). Unintended consequences: How science professors discourage women of color. *Science Education, 91*(5), 805–821.

Killpack, T. L., & Melón, L. C. (2016). Toward inclusive STEM classrooms: What personal role do faculty play? *CBE Life Sciences Education, 15*(3), 1–9.

Kozan, S., Blustein, D. L., Barnett, M., Wong, C., Conners-Kellgren, A., Haley, J., ... Wan, D. (2017). Awakening, efficacy, and action: A qualitative inquiry of social justice-infused, science education program. *Analyses of Social Issues and Public Policy, 17*(1), 205–234.

Lindemann, D., Britton, D., & Zundl, E. (2016). "I don't know why they make it so hard here": Institutional factors and undergraduate women's STEM participation. *International Journal of Gender, Science and Technology, 8*(2), 221–241.

Maton, K. I., & Hrabowski III, F. A. (2004). Increasing the number of African American PhDs in the sciences and engineering: A strengths-based approach. *American Psychologist, 59*(6), 547.

Milner, H. R., & Ford, D. Y. (2007). Underrepresentation of culturally diverse elementary students in gifted education. *Roeper Review, 29*, 166–173.

National Science Foundation, National Science Board. (2015, February 4). Revisiting the STEM workforce: A companion to Science and Engineering Indicators 2014 (NSB-2015-10). Retrieved from https://www.nsf.gov/pubs/2015/nsb201510/nsb201510.pdf

National Science Foundation, National Science Board. (2018). Science and Engineering Indicators 2018 (NSB-2018-1). Retrieved from https://www.nsf.gov/statistics/2018/nsb20181/

Ogbu, J. U. (2004). Collective identity and the burden of "acting White" in Black history, community, and education. *The Urban Review, 36*(1), 1–35.

Perna, L., Lundy-Wagner, V., Drezner, N. D., Gasman, M., Yoon, S., Bose, E., & Gary, S. (2009). The contribution of HBCU's to the preparation of African American women for STEM careers: A case study. *Research in Higher Education, 50*(1), 1–23.

Puritty, C., Strickland, L. R., Alia, E., Blonder, B., Klein, E., Kohl, M. T., ... & Gerber, L. R. (2017). Without inclusion, diversity initiatives may not be enough. *Science, 357*(6356), 1101–1102.

Schecter, D. (1991). Critical systems thinking in the 1980's: A connective summary. In R. L. Flood & M. C. Jackson (Eds.), *Critical systems thinking: Directed readings.* New York, NY: Wiley.

Shadle, S. E., Marker, A., & Earl, B. (2017). Faculty drivers and barriers: Laying the groundwork for undergraduate STEM education reform in academic departments. *International Journal of STEM Education, 4*(8), 2–13.

Shetterly, M. (2016). *Hidden figures: The American dream and the untold story of the Blackwomen mathematicians who helped win the space race.* New York, NY: HarperCollins.

Stephens, N. M., Fryberg, S. A., Markus, H. R., Johnson, C. S., & Covarrubias, R. (2012). Unseen disadvantage: How American universities' focus on independence undermines theacademic performance of first-generation college students. *Journal of Personality and Social Psychology, 102*(6), 1178.

Theokas, C., & Saaris, R. (2013). Finding America's missing AP and IB students. Retrieved from https://edtrust.org/resource/finding-americas-missing-ap-and-ib-students/

Thoman, D. B., Brown, E. R., Mason, A. Z., Harmsen, A. G., & Smith, J. L. (2015). The role of altruistic values in motivating underrepresented minority students for biomedicine. *BioScience, 65*, 183–188.

Tsui, L. (2007). Effective strategies to increase diversity in STEM fields: A review of the research literature. *The Journal of Negro Education, 76*(4), 555–581. Retrieved from www.jstor.org/stable/40037228

U.S. Department of Education (2016). STEM 2026: A vision for innovation in STEM education. Retrieved from https://innovation.ed.gov/files/2016/09/AIR-STEM2026_Report_2016.pdf

von Bertalanffy, L. (1968). *General system theory: Foundations, development, applications.* New York, NY: George Braziller.

Watson, S. L., & Watson, W. R. (2011). Critical, emancipatory, and pluralistic research for education: A review of critical systems theory. *Journal of Thought, 46*(3/4), 63. Retrieved from http://journalofthought.com/wp-content/uploads/2015/04/11watsonwatson.pdf

Whiting, G. W., & Ford, D. Y. (2009). Multicultural issues: Black students and Advanced Placement classes: Summary, concerns, and recommendations. *Gifted Child Today, 32*(1), 23–26. https://doi.org/10.4219/gct-2009-840

Wood, W. B. (2009). Innovations in teaching undergraduate biology and why we need them. *Annual Review of Cell and Developmental, 25*, 93–112.

SECTION II

MENTORING

CHAPTER 3

MENTORING FOR STEM ADVOCACY

Cameron Denson and Tamecia R. Jones
North Carolina State

PROBLEM STATEMENT

A changing economic global climate and a need to remain globally competitive in a technological world has necessitated the need to develop science, technology, engineering, and mathematics (STEM) professionals that are consistent with the nation's diverse population (Chubin, May, & Babco, 2005; Watson & Froyd, 2007; Wilson et al., 2012). Improving success and persistence in STEM for all students is critical for the nation and populous, yet diversifying the STEM fields is not only an issue of equity; diversity in STEM fields ultimately makes the profession more competent (May & Chubin, 2003; Museus, Palmer, Davis, & Maramba, 2011). If the U.S. is to continue its preeminent dominant world economy, it is incumbent upon educators to expand the diversity of the STEM talent pool (Tsui, 2007). The dawn of a new century has presented unique challenges for the nation as its predominantly White and male STEM workforce begins to age out (Aschbacher, Li, & Roth, 2010). With this fact stated, the nation must grapple with an inability of formal learning environments to effectively

---

Seeing The HiddEn Minority, pp. 39–62
Copyright © 2020 by Information Age Publishing
All rights of reproduction in any form reserved.

introduce minority students to STEM content and careers (Denson, Austin, & Hailey, 2013; Wilson et al., 2012). This inability to interest minority students in STEM content and careers is exacerbated in urban and high poverty public schools where there is a lack of resources and qualified STEM teachers (Fenzel, Domingues, & Raughly, 2006).

The challenge of meeting the nation's demand for diverse talent in STEM is underscored by the amount of money and funding invested in interventions aimed at recruiting and retaining underserved populations into STEM careers (Tsui, 2007). Turning to informal learning environments as a means of introducing students to STEM content has shown promise as a viable intervention for STEM advocacy. Informal learning environments may act as a vehicle to introduce STEM related concepts and STEM careers to students as they exist and operate outside of the normal school hours, where students spend 87% of their time (Gerber, Cavallo, & Marek, 2001). Research has provided evidence of mentorships' impact on learning (Maughan, 2006) and as an informal learning experience mentoring has shown promise as a strategy for the recruiting and retaining underserved students in STEM fields (Denson & Hill, 2010). The literature is clear that efforts to recruit and retain minority students to STEM careers should include a comprehensive approach that addresses social and psychological facets in addition to academic support (Kendricks, Nedunuri, & Arment, 2013; Wilson et al., 2012). We argue that the mentoring experience is uniquely positioned to impact learning and address issues of psychological and sociological support needed for STEM advocacy.

Before the nation can effectively begin to diversify the STEM fields several challenges need to be addressed, including; (a) current technical workforce that is undiversified in relation to the total workforce, (b) ineffective plans of action currently in use for recruitment and retention of minority students and faculty, and (c) a pedagogical approach to science, math, engineering, and technology (SMET) that is culturally unresponsive (Denson & Hill, 2010). As a multifaceted plan of action, mentoring programs have shown promise in their ability to tackle the aforementioned challenges (Campbell-Whatley, Algozzine, & Obiakor, 1997; Hall, 2006; Reddick, 2006). Seen as a tool of equity and access, mentoring programs have already benefited the growth of women and minorities in STEM professions through a myriad of practices including helping with the acclimation to the workplace environment, which traditionally has been unwelcoming to women and minorities (Hansman, 2002). Further highlighting mentorships' role and importance to diversifying STEM fields, a National Science Board report specifically recommended mentoring as a means to promote advancement in science and engineering fields (Maughan, 2006).

While the evidence of mentoring's impact on recruitment and retention is compelling, Maughan (2006) extends mentoring's capacity even further by asserting that mentoring has repeatedly shown an ability to enrich the process of learning. In fact, mentoring programs are able to distinguish themselves from other intervention programs through their emphasis on learning, which impacts both mentor and mentee through a mutual learning experience (Salinitri, 2005). Along with advising and research experiences, mentoring is identified as one of the most important predictors of academic success and persistence for underrepresented populations in STEM fields (Single, Muller, Cunningham, Single, & Carlsen, 2005). As a learning tool, mentoring may potentially be one of the most effective promotional measures in pedagogy (Stoeger, Duan, Schirner, Greindl, & Zeigler, 2013). In the context of intervention programs, mentoring is largely seen as the gold standard of pedagogy and learning and it is reported that mentored students tend to have higher GPAs, high retention rates and perform better of standardized exams (Wilson et al., 2012). In fact, a study on HBCUs that provide support programs for their students proffered that students perceived mentoring to be the biggest contributing factor to their academic success (Kendricks et al., 2013). This might be possibly due to the aspect of mentoring outcomes premised on attachment relations theory, which posits that caring is critical to social, emotional, psychological, and intellectual development (Bretherton, 1992; Watkins, 2005).

While the impact of mentoring on academic success is laudable, its most important quality may be the ability of mentoring to contribute to the emotional and psychological well being of minority and female students (Kendricks et al., 2013). Wilson et al. (2012) offers that mentoring addresses key facets of student identity and social integration into scholarship and academe as a community. Mentoring effectiveness may be due to its ability to create a unique cultural environment that supports the academic and personal growth of its participants (Tenenbaum et al., 2014). Particularly important for STEM professions is the ability of mentoring to help minorities and females develop a sense of belonging, which is particularly important for underrepresented students in STEM (Griffin, Perez, Holmes, & Mayo, 2010).

THEORETICAL FRAMEWORK

When examining issues related to race it is imperative that authors situate their argument within a theoretical framework that is bound by a set of assumptions (deMarrais & Lapa, 2004). For the purpose of this chapter authors utilized the critical race theory (CRT) as a guiding framework. CRT is a theory that acknowledges social injustice and oppressive practices; in addition, it also helps illustrate the relationship of power and culture thereby inciting awareness among the people of critical proportions

(Crenshaw, 1995). There are six unifying themes that define CRT; (1) recognition that racism is endemic, (2) expressions of skepticism toward legal claims of neutrality, objectivity, colorblindness, and meritocracy, (3) challenge a ahistoricism and a contextual analysis of the law, (4) recognition of the experiential knowledge of people of color, (5) interdisciplinary and (6) seek the elimination of racial oppression. CRT has broadly been utilized as an instrument of critique and as a framework for the investigation of legal issues concerning political, economic, and social inequalities (Stovall, 2006). However, there has been a growing interest in using this framework as a tool of critique and as an analytic tool for educational research (Lynn & Parker, 2006). Literature points to the validity of using CRT as a viable theoretical construct from which we can ascertain issues of social justice in the classroom (Dixson & Rousseau, 2005). Based on these assertions authors felt that CRT was an appropriate lens by which to understand the impact of culture and society on underrepresented students' current plight in regards to STEM fields.

BACKGROUND

The origin of the word mentoring dates back to the days of Greek mythology when Odyssey asked his female friend, the goddess of wisdom Athena, to take on the role of *Mentor* to watch over and guide his son Telemachus while he was away at sea (Hansman, 2002). This was the first record of any literature using the word *mentor,* thus beginning the ontology of the term that is used to describe beneficial people who help guide, teach and coach their protégés (Levinson, Darrow, Klein, Levinson, & McKee, 1978). While the benefits of this nebulous term have been well documented (Eby & Lockwood, 2004; Jacobi, 1991; Underhill, 2005), defining the term has been an arduous task over the years for the research field. Research pertaining to the study of mentoring unveils a plethora of differing definitions for the term based on its operational function. Levinson et al. (1978) provided one of the first general definitions of mentoring when he described its functions as that of a "teacher, sponsor, an exemplar" which begins to define the term conceptually but fails to provide any professional or personal connotation.

According to Kram (1983), mentoring is a relationship between an experienced employee and an understudy where the experienced employee acts as a role model and provides support and direction to the protégé. Conceptually, mentors may take on the role of a teacher, advisor, and a sponsor for their respective protégé (Haynes, 2004). Levinson et al. (1978) believed that the primary function of a mentor was to serve as a transitional convoy for their respective protégé. The actual act of mentoring has been known under other names including guild, artisanship, and apprenticeship. In the

Mentoring for STEM Advocacy   43

classical model of mentoring, there is typically a one-on-one interaction of unrelated individuals of different ages who network on a regular basis.

An examination of mentoring conceptualizations in organizational settings supports literature that suggests that there is a wide degree of variance in the concept, thus prompting numerous definitions. Merriam (1983) posited "Mentoring appears to mean one thing to developmental psychologists, another thing to business people and, a third thing to those in academic settings" (p. 169). Though operational definitions of mentoring vary from program to program, it is generally considered to be a relationship where a person with greater experience supports a person with less experience (Hall, 2006).

Phases of the Mentoring Relationship

Kram's (1983) seminal work on mentoring helps lay the groundwork for defining the phases of the mentoring relationship. Kram provided a study that described the phases of the mentoring program, and was able to demonstrate mentorship relationship's enormous potential to facilitate career advancements. Furthermore, Kram (1983) identified four distinct phases of this relationship to include; *initiations*—A period of six months to a year during which time the relationship gets started and begins to have importance for both managers, *cultivation*—a period of two to five years during which time the range of career and psychological functions provided expand to a maximum, *separation*—a period of six months to two years after a significant change in the structural role relationship and/or in the emotional experience of the relationship, and *redefinition*—an indefinite period after the separation phase, during which time the relationship is ended or takes on significantly different characteristics, making it a more peer-like friendship (Kram & Isabella, 1985).

Theories of Mentoring

Kram (1983) helped develop a theoretical framework for mentoring by proffering that mentoring is a relationship between an experienced member of an organization and an understudy whereby the experienced role model provides support and direction. This work was buttressed by the work of Allen and Day (2002) who postulated that through psychological support, a mentor is able to help a protégé develop a sense of competence, confidence, and self-esteem. In extending this theory there are common characteristics that are associated with mentoring such as teaching, guiding, counseling, and encouraging. Coaching is also an essential element of mentoring whose purpose is to help a younger or less experienced person develop skills, knowledge, competence, interest, or abilities in a chosen occupational field (Maughan, 2006).

To fully understand the impact of mentoring it is imperative to examine other established frameworks including social learning theories, which help explain the mentoring experience (Merriam & Caffarella, 1999). According to Merriam and Carafarella (1999) "social learning theories contribute to adult learning by highlighting the importance of social context and explicating the process of modeling and mentoring" (p. 139). Social learning theory emphasizes the point that people learn from one another and it includes the concepts of observational learning, imitation, and modeling. Bandura (1977) postulates that one mechanism by which individuals learn is observation of others individuals in their social environment. The social learning theory extends the theory of mentoring through its contention that development is achieved through observing and modeling the behaviors and attitudes of others (Ormrod, 1999). Bandura expounds upon this theory in the following quote:

> Learning would be laborious, not to mention hazardous, if people had to rely solely on the effects of their own actions to inform them what to do. Fortunately, most human behavior is learned observationally through modeling: from observing others one forms an idea of how new behaviors are performed, and on later occasions this coded information serves as a guide for action. (p. 22)

The inclusion of social learning theory to extend mentor theory is the result of social learning theory's emphasis on how social context and the environment influence and reinforces behavior (Ormond, 1999). Modeling behavior is another key aspect of social learning theory. According to Bandura (1977) social learning theory consists initially of knowledge by the individual observing a variety of models. Children repeatedly observe and learn standards and behavior patterns, not only of parents but also of siblings, peers, and other adults. After this, performance may follow, developing a pattern of behavior different from the original model (Bahn, 2001). Modeling is considered a powerful means of transmitting values, attitudes and even patterns of thought and behavior (Bandura, 1977). This sort of imitative learning is highly likely to occur when the role model (i.e., mentor) is relevant, credible, and knowledgeable, and if the behavior is rewarded by others (Eby, Lockwood, & Butts, 2005). Social learning theory is also relevant because it is seen as a bridge between behaviorist learning theories and cognitive learning theories (Ormrod, 1999). The potential of an effective mentor's influence on the behavior and perceptions of a protégé are readily apparent and coalesce with social learning theory to form an analytical lens from which to view the impact of the mentoring relationship on a student. In further explicating the mentoring experience, social cognitive career theory helps explain the link between mentoring and career success in that protégés learn and model their behavior by modeling their behavior after a senior member of an organization (Merriam & Caffarella, 1999).

Mentoring Models

It is widely accepted that although mentoring programs can be defined by their functions, the model of such a program falls within two distinct categories: informal mentoring and formal mentoring. Informal mentoring is defined as a naturally occurring relationship based on attributes, possibly similar interest and/or attraction. In this relationship the experienced member in the organization provides career and psychological support for the lesser-experienced member or protégé. In a formal mentoring relationship, the program is developed and designed by the organization to facilitate structured mentoring relationships where experienced organizational members provide career and psychological development to lesser-experienced organizational members (Haynes, 2004). In an effort to clarify the two approaches, Maughan (2006) provided a table that described the characteristics of the two mentoring models as presented in Table 3.1.

Table 3.1.
Maughan Mentoring Models

Informal Mentoring	Formal Mentoring
An unmanaged spontaneous relationship that occurs without external involvement from the organization.	Structured mentoring relationship .... with the primary purpose of systematically developing the skills and leadership abilities of less-experienced members of an organization

Researchers (Chao, Waltz, & Gardner, 1992) have suggested that informal mentoring has been more effective than formal mentoring. Due to the success of informal mentoring, many corporate, government, and private organizations have attempted to replicate this success through increased efforts to develop formal mentoring programs. Formal mentoring programs do have various obstacles to overcome, namely trying to formalize a relationship that otherwise occurs naturally between the mentor and protégé. Haynes (2004) provides a succinct and cohesive definition of the programs stating "Formal mentoring is a program designed and developed by the organization to

46　C. DENSON and T. R. JONES

facilitate structured mentoring relationships where experienced organizational members provide career and psychological development to lesser-experienced organizational members" (p. 351). Formal mentoring relationships are used extensively as a career development tool (Eby & Lockwood, 2004), which aligns well with the mission of recruiting *and* retaining minorities and women to STEM careers. A definition provided by Eby and Lockwood (2004) stated that formal mentoring refers to organizationally initiated efforts to match mentors and protégés. In this structured relationship the mentoring process is usually initiated through a third party matching process. Formal mentoring relationships are characterized by specific goals, timelines, and other guidelines as deemed necessary (Eby & Lockwood, 2004). Research has shown that there are many benefits to a well-designed formal mentoring program, some of which are unique to formal mentoring (Eby & Lockwood, 2004). In a qualitative study provided by Eby and Lockwood (2004), learning was described as the most common benefit of the mentor and protégé relationship. This is not uncommon to informal mentoring relationships but it illustrates some of the benefits for providing such a program. In examining characteristics that are unique to formal mentoring relationships it was reported that career planning was a benefit of formal mentoring that is not readily seen in informal mentoring relationships. Participants also described networking opportunities as a unique benefit of the formal mentoring relationship not to mention work role clarification, enhance job performance and a sense of pride (Eby & Lockwood, 2004).

There are many problems, revealed by research, that are common characteristics of formal mentoring programs. One of the most commonly noted issues of formal mentoring programs is mentor-protégé mismatch. The source of these mismatches can be linked to; differences in backgrounds, mismatches involved with age, interests, and/or personality (Eby & Lockwood, 2004). Difficulties in scheduling and geographic differences were duly noted as problems that were consistent with formal mentoring programs as described by Eby and Lockwood (2004). Other limitations of the formal mentoring relationship derive from a mentoring process and outcomes, which are frequently unexamined, uncritically applied, and power laden. In mentoring underrepresented populations these problems are compounded by issues of cross-gender and cross-racial mentors mentoring protégés of a different gender and/or race (Mott, 2002).

To combat the problematic nature of the formal mentoring program, scholars have suggested that formal mentoring programs imitate those of informal mentoring programs (Ellinger, 2002). This would include having mentor and protégé provide input into the pairing process thus attempting to acquiesce the need for better matching (Mott, 2002). Other frequently mentioned themes for improving the mentor-protégé relationship include;

clearer communication of program objectives, a clearly stated purpose or mission for the program, guidelines for meeting frequency, and providing guidelines for relationship length (Mott, 2002). It is recommended that mentors in formal mentoring programs receive training in order to deal with potentially challenging situations between the mentor and protégé. To deal with relationship problems it is suggested that mentors participate in interpersonal training as a way to help mentors effectively mentor their younger or less experienced colleagues (Maughan, 2006).

MENTORING IN EDUCATIONAL CONTEXTS

As described by the social cognitive theory, mentoring programs initiated within an educational context and imploring the strategies of an effective mentorship program, have the potential to greatly influence the perceptions of STEM careers for mentors and mentees (Ormrod, 1999; Tenenbaum et al., 2014). School-based mentoring programs have the potential to become part of the dynamic social reality that adolescents experience during their formative years. In a theory that extends social cognitive learning theories, the social cognitive career theory helps explain why many school-based mentoring programs have been successful in promoting career awareness and advancement (Underhill, 2005). Within educational contexts mentoring has been particularly effective in addressing the following issues for underrepresented minorities (URMs) and women: (a) lack of exposure, (b) absence of role models, and (c) difference in learning styles (Denson & Hill, 2010). Below we will look at mentoring's' role in addressing these challenges.

Absence of Role Models

The lack of minorities in technical fields has implications that reach far into our school systems. The fields of STEM, based on the demographic make-up of their correspondents, have unknowingly created barriers for underrepresented minorities (Congressional Commission on the Advancement of Women and Minorities, 2000). The Congressional Commission on the Advancement of Women and Minorities in Science, Engineering and Technology Development (2000) developed a carefully selected action-oriented design of systematic change that featured a national scope and sought to achieve immediate implementation. This legislation was developed and sponsored by Congresswoman Constance A. Morella as a way to analyze and describe the current status of women, underrepresented minorities, and persons with disabilities in the areas of STEM. Recommendations from the commission included: increased financial investments, aggressive intervention plans, adoption of high quality education standards, and a transformation of the STEM professional image (Congressional Commission on the Advancement of Women and Minorities in Science, Engineering and Technology Development, 2000). In the same report, underrepresented minorities identified barriers to careers in STEM fields which included; (a) not having an influential mentor or sponsor, and (b) lack of company role models who are members of the same racial/ethnic group. In providing a concise picture, the Congressional Commission was able to thoroughly illustrate how the lack of diversity in STEM fields acts as its own barrier to inducing diversity.

Women and underrepresented minorities often seek a high level of contact with professors of similar background and ethnic makeup often viewing them as role models and affirmation that success is possible in STEM fields (Griffin et al., 2010). In a study that examined the importance of faculty mentoring for minorities in STEM disciplines, Griffin et al. (2010) noted that participants cited various sources of support and other strategies as key to their success in STEM. These findings were consistent with other studies that highlighted the importance of mentoring and advising to the long-term success of undergraduate and graduate student development in STEM (Griffin et al., 2010; Patton 2009). As reported by Griffin et al. (2010) one of the most important contributions of these mentoring relationships is for underrepresented people "Having individuals who believe in them and their abilities" (p. 98)

With these keys to success noted, Congress has attempted to put forth legislation to meet the challenges of diversifying STEM fields. Federal legislation distinctly mentions that one purpose for mentoring is to "encourage students from underrepresented groups to pursue scientific and technical careers" (U.S. Energy Policy Act. Sec 1102, 2006, p. 10). As the nation attempts to overhaul the image of STEM and the people who go into these careers it is clear that mentoring will play a role in changing the face of STEM (Douglas, Iversen, & Kalyandurg, 2004). Formal and informal mentoring programs have been utilized for the career functions within various organizations (Eby & Lockwood, 2004) and their potential for producing palpable role models for underrepresented populations is plausible. Further research is still needed in order to understand the role of mentoring and similar outreach programs and to assess their ability to provide needed role models for underrepresented minorities.

Difference in Learning Styles

People perceive and process information differently. Each individual is unique and has a learning style to which they prescribe when processing information. A learning style can be described as a person's characteristic strengths and preferences in the ways they take in and process information. Hitch and Youatt (1995) defined learning styles as the composite of characteristic cognitive, affective and physiological factors that serve as relatively stable indicators of how learners perceive, interact with and respond to the learning environment. According to Felder and Brent (2005), these characteristics vary from person to person, and may be strong, moderate, or almost nonexistent, may change with time, and may vary from one subject or learning environment to another. Thus, it is a particular way in which an individual learns and it describes a person's typical style of thinking, remembering or problem solving.

Learning styles are important because they are important expressions of the uniqueness of an individual and specifically deal with the way individuals process information. Mentoring can potentially serve as a bridge to content for students from a variety of learning styles. Wilson et al. (2012) contends that mentoring has served as a learning tool for students and has been an effective promotional measure in pedagogy. In fact, it is reported that mentored students have higher GPAs, retention rates and perform better overall academically when compared to their non-mentored peers (Campbell-Whatley, Algozzine, & Obiakor, 1997; Hall, 2006; Wilson et al., 2012).

Pedagogically speaking there are many challenges that lie ahead for minority students in their quest for higher education, particularly in the (STEM) fields. Modern learning theories and cognitive research have made significant strides in relation to learning and effective pedagogical practices; however these advances are not particularly receptive to a diverse body of students, namely minorities. In many technological and design-based fields there is a perceived complexity in the learning environment that seems to drive women and minorities from these and related programs (DePasquale, 2003). DePasquale (2003) surmised that because of the great deal of attention on administering assignments and the grading system, little attention has been placed on the methodologies of what students learn through practice. Research within the realm of what students learn through practice may offer solutions to the many challenges that minorities face in achieving success in these design-based fields. However, this may prove difficult, for education like religion is conservative and if change does come, it will make haste very slowly (Woodson, 1933). There is no apparent protocol for how researchers should proceed to address the challenges of the underrepresentation of minorities in STEM fields but it may behoove of them to look at the history of minorities in vocational fields to discover where schools systems have seemingly failed the youth and spurned their interest in design based professions.

Early Exposure

> No one should have to wait until high school to be exposed to engineering. Early exposure to engineering will help high school students make better decisions on course selection. How many high school students do not know enough to even consider engineering as a career path, and how much of a loss is that. (p. 4)

The quote was taken from a speech given by John Brighton, Assistant Director for Engineering, National Science Foundation (Douglas, Iversen, & Kalyandurg, 2004) and was part of a keynote address that was delivered at the American Society for Engineering Education (ASEE) Leadership workshop on K–12 Engineering Outreach. His statement was a reflection of the one of the stiffest challenges that the U.S. economy is facing today, attracting students from the diverse population of U.S. citizens. K–12 STEM outreach programs have shown potential to expose many types of students to the world of engineering through partnerships and collaborations between many groups (Douglas, Iversen, & Kalyandurg, 2004) but fall short of providing a long term solution to STEM diversity. In addition, the success of peer-to-peer mentoring and informal mentoring relationships offer a pathway to introducing STEM content to underserved students at early ages.

While students might have an informal interest and even opportunities to pursue that interest, the academic trajectory for success in STEM must begin as early as possible because of the upper-level mathematics and science courses required to be admitted into undergraduate STEM programs. It should be noted that preparation impacts self-efficacy. In order to complete the upper-level mathematics courses, students must begin prerequisite subjects such as algebra in middle school. Mentors play a vital role in educating students because they can share their educational history. Interest and exposure without mentoring and advocacy to register for such classes as early as middle school still leaves students at a disadvantage for pursuing STEM careers, particularly women and minorities who might be overlooked or attend schools that have limited resources.

Another factor that mentoring may mitigate is the evolution of gender differences in science interest and mathematics from upper elementary to middle school through high school and the development of science and math identity. Girls' interest in science decrease when compared to boys as they progress through middle school (Archer et al., 2010) although they do as well as boys or better academically (Committee on Maximizing the Potential of Women in Academic Science and Engineering, 2007) and then the achievement gap grows during high school. Often, women and minorities who show interest in STEM are tokenized or stereotyped in high school (Eggleston, 2017). Having a mentor provides connection and role models (National Science Foundation, 2010) as mentors share personal stories about their professional challenges and successes (Harris, 2011).

MENTORING WOMEN AND MINORITIES

Attracting women and underrepresented minorities into STEM fields is essential to the health of the U.S. workforce (Jackson, Starobin, & Laanan, 2013). Yet these populations face very unique challenges with respect to their race, gender, and socioeconomic status (Jackson et al., 2011). In order to foster success for women and URMs in STEM it is important to face these challenges head on. It is clear that in order to deal with impending shortfalls in STEM disciplines, the U.S. needs to increase the recruitment and retention of those groups who continue to be underrepresented; women and underrepresented minorities (Tsui, 2007). Used as a tool of recruitment, mentorship programs have shown the ability to recruit and retain minorities in the workplace and positively affect students' academic success, especially for at-risk students (Allen & O'Brien, 2006; Hall, 2006). However, women and underrepresented student populations face unique challenges as students in STEM disciplines (Tsui, 2007). These challenges are exacerbated when considering the intersection of race and gender in a field that is predominately White and male (Jackson et al., 2013). For women and underrepresented student populations, issues such as campus climate and experiences around race and racism still continue to be contributing factors to their persistence or nonpersistence in STEM careers (Stoeger, Duan, Schirner, Greindl, & Ziegler, 2013). In comes mentoring which has shown promise as an intervention program for STEM advocacy for women and minorities. As part of a comprehensive approach to recruiting and retaining women and URMs, Stoeger et al. (2013) identified various aspects that they felt were necessary for effective mentoring towards STEM advocacy for women and URMs. These strategies included; (1) finding effective role models, (2) starting interventions early enough, (3) ensuring frequent interaction, (4) sharing knowledge, counseling, and guidance, (5) using numerous as well as near peer mentors, and (6) creating a STEM-friendly environment.

A challenge for both of these underrepresented groups lie in their inability to obtain mentoring due to the lack of female and minority faculty members (Tsui, 2007). Haynes (2004) contends that the lack of female and minority faculty members has led to women and URMs being less successful than their White male counterparts in acquiring mentors inside and outside of their organizations. Many have suggested that as a matter of social justice, educational policy makers should focus their efforts and legislation on developing ways to support and retain women and URMs in STEM (Hayes & Bigler, 2012). While legislative measures work their way through passage, funding, policy implementation, and sustainability, mentoring may serve as a stopgap to at least prevent URMs and women from leaving the field. Mentoring has displayed an ability to help with assimilation to the workplace for women and URMs, which bodes well for in-service practitioners (Hansman, 2002; Van Collie, 1998).

Although it is true that STEM cultural climates have improved over the years, there are still many challenges those students pursuing careers in STEM face on a daily basis. The focus on underrepresented student groups invites a need to address identity issues and changing the perception of a field in which many underrepresented students have a hard time identifying. The mentoring experience helps builds upon Lave and Wenger's (1999) community of practice, which places an emphasis on identity. It is proffered that membership into a particular community translates into an identity as a source of competence (Lave & Wenger, 1999), which lends some insight into the difficulty of mentoring women and minorities in STEM.

Mentoring Women in STEM

While it is true that women and minorities face similar barriers in the pursuit of STEM careers, there are notable differences that deserve considerable research attention on their own (Tsui, 2007). A lack of equitable participation of women in STEM at all levels has helped contribute to many issues including, lower salaries, more limited career opportunities, and a lack of viable roles models (Stoeger et al., 2013). Discrimination may help explain the underrepresentation of women in STEM as they are perpetuated through gender stereotypes that favor men's work personality over women (Hayes & Bigler, 2012). One of the most influential differences between women and URMs lie in what Eccles (1983) refers to as differing work-related values which translates to gender differentiated academic values (Hayes & Bigler, 2013). Preliminary research in this area reveal that effective mentoring practices include valuing and showing support and appreciation for individual's talent and contributions and having a mentor who believes in the mentees' abilities and recognition of talent (Hayes & Bigler, 2012). Moving forward, future research on mentoring should focus their attention towards gender differentiation of occupational values (Hayes & Bigler, 2012; Stroeger et al., 2013).

In looking to explain the underrepresentation of women in STEM fields, many concerns are centered on the issue of discrimination and research has helped illuminate damaging stereotypes of STEM ability which favor men over women (Hayes & Bigler, 2012). This is cultivated through environmental and societal factors that are primarily responsible for deterring women from entering or persisting in STEM (Single et al., 2005). While mentoring has displayed the ability to sustain girls' interest in STEM (Stoeger, Hopp, & Ziegler, 2017), these experiences are less readily available to women students (Single et al., 2005). There has been some promise in the area of distance mentoring or e-mentoring which studies indicate is an appropriate measure for promoting women's development in STEM (Stoeger et al., 2013). In fact, online mentoring or e-mentoring has been particularly useful for building and sustaining interest in STEM fields for females at the secondary level (Stoeger, et al., 2017). Yet, when establishing mentoring efforts focused on women in STEM there are many factors that need to be considered. First, successful female role models are vital to supporting women in STEM. In addition, intervention programs should reach females at an early age before their interest in STEM begins to dissipate. Furthermore, studies have indicated that successful mentoring programs for women should emphasize the regularity and frequency of the mentor-mentee relationship (Stoeger et al., 2017).

FUTURE OF MENTORING IN STEM

Online mentoring or its more colloquial phrasing of e-mentoring is seen as a special form of mentoring in which at least some of the communication takes place electronically (Stoeger et al., 2017). This mentoring is "a computer mediated, mutually beneficial relationship between a mentor and a protégé which provides learning, advising, encouraging, promoting, and modeling, that is often boundary-less, egalitarian, and qualitatively different than face-to-face mentoring" (Bierema & Merriam, 2002, p. 214.) Single and Muller (1999) define electronic mentoring or e-mentoring as

> a naturally occurring relationship or a paired relationship within a program that is established between a more senior individual (mentor) and a lesser skilled or experienced individual (protégé), primarily using electronic communications, and is intended to develop and grow the skills, knowledge, confidence, and cultural understanding of the lesser skilled individual to help him or her succeed. (p. 236)

The earliest e-mentoring is noted as being limited to elite scientists through e-mail and the World Wide Web but had become ubiquitous on college campuses by the late 1990s. Lenear (2007) further identifies e-mail, the Internet, telephone, fax, discussion conferencing, and video conferencing as communication media used in e-mentoring environments.

E-mentoring is a helpful alternative to face-to-face mentoring due to its ability to overcome logistical barriers to the mentoring relationship. What cannot be disputed is the role of e-mentoring in creating competencies for the current STEM labor market (Martin, Platis, Malita, & Ardeleanu, 2011). E-mentoring is effective in cultivating the professional profile of future STEM workers, contributes to creating skills and practical abilities of the mentee and aids in knowledge transfer of inexperienced employees (Martin et al., 2011). The continued advancements of computer-mediated communications (CMC) have provided a platform for mentoring at a distance. E-mentoring presents an opportunity to provide experiences and support while overcoming logistical obstacles for mentors and mentees. Seen as a practical, creative and cost effective alternative to face-to-face mentoring, e-mentoring offers benefits similar to more traditional modalities, including the ability to improve professional identity development (Ghods & Boyce, 2013).

Although limited, there is a body of literature that speaks to the success of virtual mentoring experiences, particularly for college students working with professionals (Hixenbaugh, Dewart, Drees, & Williams, 2006; Wilburn, Amer, & Kilpatrick, 2009). Additionally, the literature has provided evidence on the ability of e-mentoring to impact individuals in the workplace (Dappen & Iserhagen, 2002). More importantly, the study found statistically significant difference in levels of satisfaction for students who come from a demographic that is underrepresented for the engineering profession (Muller & Barrison, 2003). There is also research that speaks to the benefits of e-mentoring for undergraduate students when paired with upperclassmen and graduate mentors (Cascio & Gasker, 2001; Hixenbaugh et al., 2006). However, much of the literature surrounding the benefits of e-mentoring is mostly anecdotal and qualitative in nature, as noted by Ghods and Boyce (2013), which highlights the need for rigorous research on e-mentoring.

Ghods and Boyce (2013) contend that e-mentoring is uniquely suited for addressing social inequities by providing mentoring opportunities to those who would not otherwise receive them due to geography, costs, and/ or physical limitations. Additionally, study results indicate that e-mentoring is an appropriate measure for promoting girl's development in STEM (Stoeger et al., 2013). In addressing issues of resources and access, Brown and Adler (2008) contend that the Internet can provide students with access to high-powered software and tools, such as telescopes, and supercomputer simulation models. Recently, advances in educational and instructional technology have allowed for the merging of the Internet-based virtual world and the physical world thus allowing for the extension of traditional learning (U.S. Department of Education, 2017). Utilizing the powerful tool of the Internet with the theoretical underpinnings of a formal mentorship program may provide learning experiences that extend beyond the traditional classroom. In addition, the convenience of using mobile and web-based technology to facilitate an e-mentoring experience helps eliminate many logistical challenges of maintaining a meaningful relationship. This is particularly beneficial for student mentors in STEM disciplines where many must contend with demanding schedules and rigorous coursework.

CONCLUSION

Due to challenges inherent in our modern school system, numerous students, especially underrepresented youth, require enhanced support and better assistance than those presently offered (Hall, 2006). For underserved students who have an interest in STEM careers, mentoring serves as a viable means of introducing them to STEM careers and enhancing their learning experience (Hall, 2006; Kendricks et al., 2013). The literature is replete with studies documenting the need for the U.S. to develop a workforce more reflective of its general population in order to meet the need for world-class talent in STEM (Chubin, May, & Babco, 2005; Watson & Froyd, 2007). This revelation speaks to the importance of funding and supporting programs that promote awareness and interest in STEM fields. Currently, the attrition rate for students pursuing careers in STEM disciplines is outpacing the need and demand for STEM professionals (Wilson et al., 2012); highlighting the need for universities across the nation to look for and develop effective ways to promote diversity and increase the recruitment and retention of URMs to STEM careers (Kendricks et al., 2013). The research has clearly documented the ability of mentoring to positively impact students' attitudes, achievement, and rates of graduation (Dappen & Isernhagen, 2002; Hall, 2006). What is also evident is mentorings' ability to increase enrollment and retention for minority students as well as impact their academic achievement in STEM disciplines (Kendrick et al., 2013).

In addressing the theoretical framework guiding this work, CRT as a theory implies that racism and stereotyping has indubitably contributed to manifestations of group advantage and jettisons the notion of colorblindness (Dixson & Rousseau, 2005). Acknowledging these factors is vital when attempting to develop interventions that purport to address shortcoming in STEM fields. Like the myriad disciplines that make up STEM fields, CRT is by nature interdisciplinary and applicable across the vast professions of STEM. The long history of underrepresentation by underserved populations in STEM fields highlight a greater issue of equal opportunity and cultural relevance. With this noted, mentoring is uniquely positioned to address these shortcoming using a model that has proven to be effective in not only addressing academic needs but social and psychological ones as well (Kendricks et al., 2013).

A review of literature on informal learning environments shows that mentorship programs provide some of the best answers to the question of recruit and retaining underrepresented students in STEM fields (Denson & Hill, 2010). It is clearly evident that if the U.S. is to maintain its competitive edge in the global economy then mentoring will play a crucial role in addressing the nation's need and demand for more diverse talent in STEM. This chapter has attempted to illustrate the importance of mentoring for STEM advocacy and provide examples of mentoring's past success. However, in going forward mentoring must adapt to a new generation of learners and the unique challenges of mentoring women and underrepresented populations. With this said, institutions of higher learning must enact concerted efforts to recruit, attract, and sustain faculty who are women and come from underrepresented populations. As a testament to this claim, a study by Hayes and Bigler (2012) identified that perception of one's mentor values and support of a student was a strong predictor of success in STEM work. In fact, the most important factor in diversifying the STEM fields may lie in its ability to attract more women to the profession. While it is true that one of the most critical factors that contribute to success for women in STEM fields is the mentoring from experienced faculty members (Hayes & Bigler, 2012), both men and women reported higher levels of support from their *female* mentors in comparison to male mentors (Stoeger et al., 2013).

As an intervention plan, mentoring has displayed the ability to potentially be one of the most effective promotional measures in pedagogy (Stoeger et al. 2013). It is seen as the gold standard of pedagogy and learning for intervention programs with mentored students reporting having higher GPAs and higher retention rates (Wilson et al., 2012). Even more importantly, mentoring contributes to personal, educational and professional growth for mentees *and* their mentors (Kendricks et al., 2013). This ultimately leads to increased interest and engagement for all those vying for STEM careers. Still more work is needed in the area of mentoring for STEM advocacy. First, for mentoring to be effective, ultimately it should start at earlier and earlier ages (Stoeger et al., 2017). In addition, the success of the mentoring relationship is contingent upon having quality mentors, which speaks to the importance of mentor training. Furthermore, the importance of quality mentor-mentee matching cannot be understated (Stoeger et al., 2013).

The advent of technology and innovative teaching practices has extended mentoring capabilities; this is true particularly for underrepresented minorities and women. For underrepresented students who lack access and institutional partnerships, Ghods and Boyce (2013) contend that e-mentoring is uniquely suited for addressing social inequities by providing mentoring opportunities to those who would not otherwise receive them due to geography, costs, and/or physical limitations. Future research efforts should focus on funding and support of innovative mentoring models that can provide empirical data, which helps provide valuable insight into best practices for mentoring for STEM advocacy. The lack of comparative studies in this realm suggests that many findings in this area may have exaggerated the actual effectiveness of mentorship programs (Underhill, 2005).

REFERENCES

Allen, T.D., & Day, R. (2002). The relationship between career motivation and self-efficacy with protégé career success. *Journal of Vocational Behavior, 64*(1), 72–91.

Allen, T. D., Eby, L. T., Poteet, M. L., Lentz, E., & Lima, L. (2004). Career benefits associated with mentoring for protégés: A meta-analysis. *Journal of applied psychology, 89*(1), 127.

Allen, T. D., & O'Brien, K. E. (2006). Formal mentoring programs and organizational attraction. *Human Resource Development Quarterly, 17*(1), 43–58.

Aschbacher, P. R., Li, E., & Roth, E. J. (2010). Is science me? High school students' identities, participation and aspirations in science, engineering, and medicine. *Journal of Research in Science Teaching, 47*(5), 564–582.

Archer, L., DeWitt, J., Osborne, J., Dillon, J., Willis, B., & Wong, B. (2010). "Doing" science versus "being" a scientist: Examining 10/11-year-old schoolchildren's constructions of science through the lens of identity. *Science Education, 94*(4), 617–639. doi:10.1002/sce.20399

Bandura, A. (1977). *Social learning theory.* New York, NY: General Learning Press.

Bahn, D. (2001). Social learning theory: Its application in the context of nurse education. *Nurse Education Today, 21,* 110–117.

Bierema, L. L., & Merriam, S. B. (2002). E-mentoring: Using computer mediated communication to enhance the mentoring process | Springer Link. *Innovative Higher Education, 26*(3), 211–227. doi:10.1023/a:1017921023103

Bretherton, I. (1992). The origins of attachment theory: John Bowlby and Mary Ainsworth. *Developmental Psychology, 28*(5), 759–775.

Brown, S.J., & Adler, R. P. (2008). Open education, the long tail, and learning 2.0. *Educause Review, 43*(1), 16–20.

Campbell-Whatley, G. D., Algozzine, B., & Obiakor, F. (1997). Using mentoring to improve academic programming for African American male youths with mild disabilities. *The School Counselor, 44*(5), 362–367.

Cascio, T., & Gasker, J. (2001). Everyone has a shining side: Computer-mediated mentoring in social work education. *Journal of Social Work Education, 37*(2), 283–293.

58 C. DENSON and T. R. JONES

Chubin, D. E., May, G. S., & Babco, E. L. (2005). Diversifying the engineering workforce. *Journal of Engineering Education, 94*(1), 73–86.

Committee on Maximizing the Potential of Women in Academic Science and Engineering. (2007). *Beyond bias and barriers: Fulfilling the potential of women in academic science and engineering.* Washington, DC: National Academies Press.

Congressional Commission on the Advancement of Women and Minorities in Science, Engineering and Technology Development. (2000, September). Land of plenty: Diversity as America's competitive edge in science, engineering and technology. Retrieved April 1, 2018, from http://www.nsf.gov/od/cawmset/

Crenshaw, K. (1995). *Critical race theory: The key writings that formed the movement.* New York, NY: The New Press.

Chao, G., Walz, P., & Gardner, P. (1992). Formal and informal mentorships. *Personnel Psychology, 45,* 619–636.

Dappen, L., & Isernhagen, J. C. (2002). TeamMates: A model to support mentoring in rural schools. *Journal of Research in Rural Education, 17*(3), 154–161.

deMarrais, K., & Lapan, S. D. (2004). *Handbook of qualitative research* (2nd ed.) London, England: SAGE.

Denson, C. D., Austin, C., & Hailey, C. (2013, June). *Evaluating the impact of the engineering self-efficacy, interests, and perceptions survey.* Paper presented at the meeting of the American Society for Engineering Education, Atlanta, GA.

Denson, C. D., & Hill, R. B. (2010). Impact of an engineering mentorship program on African-American male high school students' perceptions and self-efficacy. *Journal of Industrial Teacher Education, 47*(1), 99–127.

DePasquale, P. J. (2003). Implications of the learning of programming through the implementation of subsets in program development environment (Doctoral dissertation), Virginia Polytechnic Institute and State University. Retrieved March 27, 2006, from *Journal of Technology Education* Masterfile database. Retrieved from https://vtechworks.lib.vt.edu/handle/10919/28367

Dixson, A. D., & Rousseau, C. K. (2005). And we are still not saved: Critical race theory in education ten years later. *Race Ethnicity and Education, 8*(1), 7–27.

Douglas, J., Iversen, E., & Kalyandurg, C. (2004). Engineering in the K–12 classroom: An analysis of current practices & guidelines for the future. Retrieved March 28, 2006 from *Journal of Technology Education* Masterfile database. Retrieved from http://teachers.egfi-k12.org/wp-content/uploads/2010/01/Engineering_in_the_K-12_Classroom.pdf

Eby, L. T., & Lockwood, A. (2004). Protégé and mentors reactions to participating in formal mentoring programs: A qualitative investigation. *Journal of Vocational Behavior, 67*(3), 441–458.

Eccles, J. S. (1983). Expectancies, values, and academic behaviors. In J. T. Spence (Ed.), *Achievement and achievement motives: Psychological and sociological approaches* (pp. 75–146). San Francisco, CA: Free Man.

Ellinger, A. D. (2002). Mentoring in contexts: The workplace and educational institutions. In C. Hansman, V., Mott, A. D. Ellinger, & T. Guy (Eds.), *Critical perspectives on Mentoring: Trends and Issues, ERIC Info Series No. 388.* Ohio, Japan: ERIC Clearinghouse on adult, career, and vocational education, Ohio State university; 2002:15-26.

Eby, L.T., Lockwood, A.L., & Butts, M. (2005). Perceived support for mentoring: A multiple perspectives approach. *Journal of Vocational Behavior, 68*(2), 267–291.

Eggleston, S. R. (2017). *The K–12 experiences of African American collegiate women in STEM majors: A counter narrative* (Doctor of Philosophy), North Carolina State University, Raleigh, NC. (10610703)

Felder, R. M., & Brent, R. (2005). Understanding student differences. *Journal of Engineering Education, 94*(1), 57–72.

Fenzel, L. M., Domingues, J., & Raughley, B. C. (2006). Educating at-risk urban African American children: A comparison of two types of middle schools. *Online Submission*. Retrieved from files.eric.ed.gov/fulltext/ED497444.PDF

Gerber, B. L., Cavallo, A. M., & Marek, E. A. (2001). Relationships among informal learning environments, teaching procedures and scientific reasoning ability. *International Journal of Science Education, 23*(5), 535–549.

Ghods, N., & Boyce, C. (2013). Virtual coaching and mentoring. In J. Passmore, D. B. Peterson, T. Freire (Eds), *The Wiley-Blackwell handbook of the psychology of coaching and mentoring* (pp. 501–523). Hoboken, NJ: John Wiley & Sons.

Griffin, K. A., Perez, D., Holmes, A. P., & Mayo, C. E. (2010). Investing in the future: The importance of faculty mentoring in the development of students of color in STEM. *New Directions for Institutional Research, 2010*(148), 95–103.

Hall, H. R. (2006). *Mentoring young men of color: Meeting the needs of African American and Latino students.* Blue Ridge Summit, PA: Rowman & Littlefield Education.

Hansman, C. A. (2002). Diversity and power in mentoring relationships. *Critical Perspectives on Mentoring: Trends and Issues,* 39–48.

Harris, J. (2011). Designs for curriculum-based telementoring. In D. A. Scigliano (Ed.), *Online communication technologies for learning.* Pittsburgh, PA: IGI Global.

Hayes, A. R., & Bigler, R. S. (2013). Gender-related values, perceptions of discrimination, and mentoring in STEM graduate training. *International Journal of Gender, Science and Technology, 5*(3), 254–280.

Haynes, R. K. (2004, March 3–7). *A summary analysis and prescriptions for mentoring in multicultural organizations. Online Submission.* Paper presented at the Academy of Human Resource Development International Conference (AHRD), Austin, TX.

Hitch, E. J., & Youatt, J. P. (1995). *Communicating family and consumer sciences: A guidebook for professionals.* South Holland, IL: Goodheart-Willcox.

Hixenbaugh, P., Dewart, H., Drees, D., & Williams, D. (2006). Peer e-mentoring: Enhancement of the first year experience. *Psychology Learning & Teaching, 5*(1), 8–14.

Jackson, D. L., Starobin, S. S., & Laanan, F. S. (2013). The shared experiences: Facilitating successful transfer of women and underrepresented minorities in STEM fields. *New Directions for Higher Education, 2013*(162), 69–76.

Jacobi, M. (1991). Mentoring and undergraduate academic success: A literature review. *Review of educational research, 61*(4), 505–532.

Kram, K. E. (1983). Phases of the mentor relationship. *Academy of Management Journal, 26*(4), 608–625.

Kram, K. E., & Isabella, L. A. (1985). Mentoring alternatives: The roles of peer relationships in career development. *The Academy of Management Journal, 28*(1), 110–132.

Kendricks, K. D., Nedunuri, K. V., & Arment, A. R. (2013). Minority student perceptions of the impact of mentoring to enhance academic performance in STEM disciplines. *Journal of STEM Education: Innovations and Research, 14*(2), 38.

Lave, J., & Wenger, E. (1999). Learning and pedagogy in communities of practice. In J. Leach & B. Moon (Eds.), *Learners and pedagogy* (pp. 21–33). London, England: Paul Chapman.

Lenear, P. E. (2007). E-mentoring interaction models. *Online Submission*. Retrieved from https://pdfs.semanticscholar.org/0bd3/d83b867e42960f224a2e3fd2a397a7147251.pdf

Levinson, D. J., Darrow C. N., Klein E. B., Levinson M. H., & McKee, B. (1978). *The seasons of a man's life*. New York, NY: Alfred A. Knopf.

Lynn, M., & Parker, L. (2006). Critical race studies in education: Examining a decade of research on U.S. schools. *The Urban Review, 38*(4), 257–290.

Martin, C., Platis, M., Malita, L., & Ardeleanu, M. (2011). The role of EMENTORING and social media for developing the entrepreneurship competences. *Procedia-Social and Behavioral Sciences, 15*, 947–951.

Maughan, B. D. (2006). *Mentoring among scientists: implications of interpersonal relationships within a formal mentoring program* (No. INL/CON-06-11721). Idaho National Laboratory (INL).

May, G. S., & Chubin, D. E. (2003). A retrospective on undergraduate engineering success for underrepresented minority students. *Journal of Engineering Education, 92*(1), 27–39.

Merriam, S.B. (1983). Mentor and protégé: A critical review of the literature. *Adult Education Quarterly, 33*(3), 161–73.

Merriam, S. B., & Caffarella, R.S. (1999). *Learning in adulthood*. San Francisco, CA: Jossey-Bass.

Mott, V. W. (2002). *Mentoring: From Athena to the 21st century*. Eric Clearinghouse on Adult, Career, and Vocational Education.

Muller, C. B., & Barsion, S. J. (2007). *Assessment of a large-scale e-mentoring network for women in engineering and science: Just how good is MentorNet?* Washington, DC: Women in Engineering ProActive Network.

Museus, S. D., Palmer, R. T., Davis, R. J., & Maramba, D. (Eds.). (2011). Racial and ethnic minority student success in STEM education. *ASHE Higher Education Report, 36*(6), 1–140

National Science Foundation. (2010). *Preparing the next generation of STEM innovators: Identifying and developing our nation's human capital*. Arlington, VA: National Science Foundation.

Ormund, J. E. (1999). *Human learning*. Upper Saddle River, NJ: Prentice-Hall.

Patton, L. D. (2009). My sister's keeper: A qualitative examination of mentoring experiences among African American women in graduate and professional schools. *The Journal of Higher Education, 80*(5), 510–537.

Ragins, B. R., & Scandura, T. A. (1999). Burden or blessing? Expected costs and benefits of being a mentor. *Journal of Organizational Behavior: The International Journal of Industrial, Occupational and Organizational Psychology and Behavior, 20*(4), 493–509.

Reddick, R. J. (2006). The gift that keeps giving: Historically Black college and university-educated scholars and their mentoring at predominately White institutions. *The Journal of Educational Foundations*, *20*(1/2), 61.

Salinitri, G. (2005). The effects of formal mentoring on the retention rates for first-year, low achieving students. *Canadian Journal of Education/Revue canadienne de l'education*, *28*(4), 853–873.

Single, P. B., & Muller, C. B. (1999). Electronic mentoring: Issues to advance research and practice. *Presented in International Mentoring Association Annual Meeting*. Retrieved from learntechlib.org/p/88219/

Single, P. B., Muller, C. B., Cunningham, C. M., Single, R. M., & Carlsen, W. S. (2005). Mentornet: E-mentoring for women students in engineering and science. *Journal of Women and Minorities in Science and Engineering*, *11*(4), 60.

Stoeger, H., Duan, X., Schirner, S., Greindl, T., & Ziegler, A. (2013). The effectiveness of a one-year online mentoring program for girls in STEM. *Computers & Education*, *69*, 408–418.

Stoeger, H., Hopp, M., & Ziegler, A. (2017). Online mentoring as an extracurricular measure to encourage talented girls in STEM: An empirical study of one-on-one versus group mentoring. *Gifted Child Quarterly*, *61*(3), 239–249.

Stovall, D. (2006). Forging community in race and class: Critical race theory and the quest for social justice in education. *Race ethnicity and Education*, *9*(3), 243–259.

Tenenbaum, L. S., Anderson, M. K., Jett, M., & Yourick, D. L. (2014). An innovative near-peer mentoring model for undergraduate and secondary students: STEM focus. *Innovative Higher Education*, *39*(5), 375–385.

Tsui, L. (2007). Effective strategies to increase diversity in STEM fields: A review of the research literature. *The Journal of Negro Education*, *76*(4), 555–581

Underhill, C. M. (2005). The effectiveness of mentoring programs in corporate settings: A meta-analytical review of the literature. *Journal of Vocational Behavior*, *68*(2), 292–307.

U.S. Department of Education (2017). "Infrastructure: Access and Enable." Retrieved from http://tech.ed.gov/netp/infrastructure-access-and-enable/

U.S. Energy Policy Act. (2006). 109th Congress, 1st Session. Retrieved November 8, 2017, from http://frwebgate.access.gpo.gov/cgibin/getdoc.cgi?dbname=109_cong_bills&docid=f:h6pcs.txt.pdf

Van Collie, S. C. (1998). Moving up through mentoring. *Workforce*. Retrieved from https://www.questia.com/magazine/1P3-27007387/moving-up-through-mentoring

Watkins, P. G. H. (2005). *Mentoring in the scientific disciplines: Presidential Awards for Excellence in Science, Mathematics, and Engineering Mentoring*. Claremont, California, Claremont Graduate University.

Watson, K., & Froyd, J. (2007). Diversifying the US engineering workforce: A new model. *Journal of Engineering Education*, *96*(1), 19–32.

Wilburn, N. L., Amer, T. S., & Kilpatrick, B. G. (2009). Establishing an eMentor program: Increasing the interaction between accounting majors and professionals. In *Advances in Accounting Education* (pp. 27–59). Bingley, UK: Emerald Group Publishing Limited.

Wilson, Z. S., Holmes, L., Sylvain, M. R., Batiste, L., Johnson, M., McGuire, S. Y., & Warner, I. M. (2012). Hierarchical mentoring: A transformative strategy for improving diversity and retention in undergraduate STEM disciplines. *Journal of Science Education and Technology, 21*(1), 148–156.

Woodson, C. G. (1933). *The mis-education of the Negro*. Chicago, IL: African American Images.

CHAPTER 4

DIFFERENT WORLDS

A Picture of STEM Mentorships at PWIs and HBCUs

Daniel Alston
University of North Carolina, Charlotte

Brandi Copeland-Kamp
Clemson University

In order to maintain its authority in science and technology, the U.S. is in need of more individuals who can work in science, technology, engineering, and mathematics (STEM) fields. College graduation metrics show that 300,000 STEM degrees are awarded annually from colleges and universities in the United States; however, researchers project a need for a 34% annual increase in the amount of STEM undergraduate degrees conferred to meet the increasing demand of jobs in these sectors (President's Council of Advisors on Science and Technology [PCAST], 2012). Given the need for a 34% annual job demand increase, colleges and universities need to attract and retain more students into STEM programs. To date, Black students are a reservoir of potential human capital that has yet to be fully accessed. Low

---

Seeing The HiddEn Minority, pp. 63–81
Copyright © 2020 by Information Age Publishing
All rights of reproduction in any form reserved.

enrollment and retention of Black students in STEM undergraduate and postgraduate degrees is an issue highlighted by researchers (Myers & Pavel, 2011). While awareness of this problem has heightened, Black students are still vastly underrepresented when it comes to graduation rates and job placements in STEM fields (Chen, Ingram, & Davis, 2014).

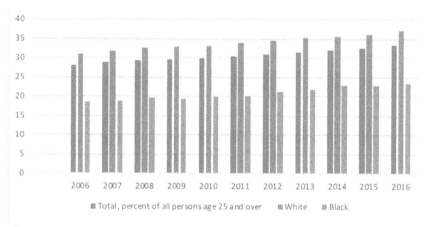

Figure 4.1. Bachelor's degree Attainment at Age 25+.

Figure 4.1 shows the rate of bachelor's degree attainment for the entire American population, followed by a breakdown of White and Black graduates from 2006 to 2016. Although there is a general trend upwards, the gap between White and Black populations who have earned a bachelor's degree has increased. The gap grows from 12.4 percentage points in 2006 to 13.8 percentage points by 2016 (Education Department, 2018). Bachelor's degrees conferred to Black students in 2015 accounted for 192,715 degrees, only 22,533 of which were in STEM fields (U.S. Department of Education, 2017). To simplify, Black students received 7.1% of all STEM bachelor's degrees in 2015, while White students received 65.8%. Experts agree there is an unequal representation of Black college graduates, particularly in STEM fields (Chen, Ingram & Davis, 2014). Shown by the NCES data above, this unequal representation has resulted in a large discrepancy in the percentage of degree holders by race.

Given the data on the differences between race and degrees conferred, recruiting Black students into STEM programs is important. Further, retention in and completion of STEM degrees is also a goal of colleges and universities (Slovacek et al., 2011). There are several factors responsible for increasing the retention rate of Black students in STEM programs. Engaging students in research experiences develops a sense of belonging and increases understanding of what it is like to work in a specified STEM

Different Worlds 65

field. This sense of belonging and increased understanding encourages students to continue in their program of study (Hernandez, Schultz, Estrada, Woodcock, & Chance, 2013). Another factor facilitating the retention of students in STEM programs is the accessibility of instruction which supplements in-class teaching. The effect of this factor was especially noticeable for underrepresented minorities (Peterfreund, Rath, Xenos, & Bayliss, 2008). Financial support is also a crucial factor in student retention (Slovacek et al., 2011) and while underrepresented minorities are more likely to receive financial aid, this financial air is on average less than Caucasian or Asian students (National Science Foundation [NSF], 2003).

Mentoring, the foundation of this chapter, is another key factor that increases Black students' retention in STEM programs. While researchers define mentoring in a variety of ways, Tillman (2001) provides a holistic definition of mentoring. In Tillman's words mentoring is a

> process within a contextual setting; a relationship between a more experienced individual; a means for professional networking, counseling, guiding, instructing, modeling, and sponsoring; a developmental mechanism (personal, professional and psychological); a socialization and reciprocal relationship; and an opportunity for identity transformation for both the mentor and the protégé. (p. 296)

For Black students enrolled in STEM programs, mentoring is a major contributor to student retention and success (Carter, Mandell, & Maton, 2009; McCoy, Winkle-Wagner, & Luedke, 2015; Slovacek et al., 2011). According to Hill, Pettus, and Hedin (1990) mentoring is the most critical factor in Black students choosing a career in a science-related field. This is partially due to mentors being able to induct and socialize students into the community related to their field of study. Further, mentors can function to serve as role models and career inspiration and provide psychological support to their mentees. Because researchers have noted the many positive effects of mentoring, it is no surprise that mentoring takes place at predominantly white institutions (PWIs) and historically Black colleges and universities (HBCUs). However, the cultures of these institutions can impact the trajectory of mentor relationships.

Cultural Differences Between HBCUs and PWIs

According to the National Center for Education Statistics (NCES), there are currently 112 accredited HBCUs left in America. This number is miniscule when compared to the 4,724 degree granting institutions that were identified during the 2013–2014 school term (U.S. Department of Education, 2016). In 2015, HBCUs served 1.6% of all college students and 10.6% of all Black students (NCES, 2017). Further, HBCUs serve approximately five times the expected number of Black students in the United States. Therefore, one of the most obvious differences between HBCUs and PWIs is their racial makeup (Palmer & Wood, 2012; Wei & Hendrix, 2016). HBCUs have a large Black student population and PWIs are predominantly White. This racial make-up also extends to the respective faculty and the leadership. Even though leadership at PWIs expresses desires to be inclusive of all cultures, the culture that is most rewarded via policies and other means is White culture (Wei & Hendrix, 2016). In contrast, HBCUs were developed with the express purpose of educating and promoting the culture, values, and identities of Black students.

Researchers note there is a difference in the culture of learning between PWIs and HBCUs. One Black professor espoused the high-end energy of African Americans and how this contributed to a collaborative learning environment; "We [African Americans] have a very high-end energy type of environment when we're at home, a lot of singing, and a lot dancing" (Wei & Hendrix, 2016, p. 106). Given the home culture of African Americans is centered on interaction, including interaction in the education of African Americans is important. Glocke (2016) describes a high-end energy class as discussion based, communal and collective, and inclusive. In order to achieve a class that exhibits the descriptors listed above, Glocke uses small and big circles for group discussion, group projects and presentations, communal quizzes and tests, flexible lesson plans and curricula to provide freedom for discussion and student interests, and zero tolerance for disrespect toward diversity. On the other hand, a White professor who was interviewed placed more focus on orderly classroom conduct, such as hand raising in developing a productive classroom culture (Wei & Hendrix, 2016). This type of practice is more individual in nature and suggests an environment where the teacher is in control of the conversation. Glocke refers to the aforementioned learning environment as being hierarchical, competitive, capitalist, and individualistic. Further, these individualistic learning environments have the potential to stifle energy and interaction amongst students.

The culture at HBCUs is often referred to as familial. The trend of home culture metaphors, such as analogies to family units, is reported regularly within literature about HBCUs (Flowers, Scott, Riley, & Palmer, 2015; Wei & Hendrix, 2016). A student described faculty-student relationships at HBCUs as a parental-offspring dynamic (Wei & Hendrix, 2016). This has also been referred to as "other-mothering" (Flowers et al., 2015; Goings, 2017). This term was coined from the observation of the extraordinary attention that black female professors give their students.

Other-mothering is a term used to describe the phenomenon of "women who assist blood-mothers by sharing mothering responsibilities (Collins,

2000, p. 178). Other-mothering was a practice often exhibited by African American communities during slavery due to children being separated from their mothers by death or the selling process. As formal education was prohibited to slaves, other-mothering also encompassed the informal education and socialization of orphaned slave children (Dubey, 1995; Perkins, 1989). Thus, other-mothering was influential in uplifting the Black community. Researchers (e.g., Case, 1997) have found that other-mothering occurs in formal education settings and extends to male, as well as female African American educators. While critical in the days of slavery, the practice of other-mothering has continued and supports the familial environment at HBCUs.

Along with the close attention paid to students (i.e., other-mothering) comes the knowledge of their lived experiences (Palmer & Wood, 2012). Having and understanding the knowledge of Black students' lived experiences cultivates a supportive environment at HBCUs that is often missing for Black students at PWIs. It has been reported that PWI professors tend to see all Black students as a homogenous group, while being more sensitive to the variability inherent of their White counterparts. Palmer and Wood (2012) argue the diversity of Black male students, specifically, spans challenges that range from men who are gay, men who are athletes, men who are in STEM to men who are a part of a Greek orgnaization, to name a few. Some of this diversity is not readily apparent to those who have had little in-depth experiences with Black communities. This can lead to PWIs having a culture that is less than welcoming to Black students, as well as professors who hold stereotypical beliefs about Black students (Guiffrida, 2005). Next, we will explore what contributes to the differences in culture between PWIs and HBCUs and how this difference has been propagated and sustained.

Keeping Us Hidden: The Impact of Institutionalized Racism on Institutional Culture

Institutionalized racism is not a new phenomenon. Researchers have spent time explaining what it is, where it takes place and how it impacts the trajectory of Black students. While institutional racism impacts the retention rate of Black students—to be discussed in the paragraphs to follow—it also negatively impacts the enrollment of Black students in colleges and universities and in STEM programs. Researchers have explained how various factors (e.g., testing bias of the SAT and ACT, lower opportunities for Black students to learn, systematic disinvestment from black communities) can lead to Black students having lower admittance rates into colleges and universities (Feagin, 2014; Waymer & Street, 2016).

Institutionalized racism can also impact the retention rate and completion of college degrees for Black students through other less visible factors. School policies are one such form of institutionalized racism that may be particularly hard to overcome, as "those with access to resources are able to create policy which privileges their standing in the social order while diminishing the standing of those without access to resources" (Jones, 2013, p. 131). Many of these policies become normalized and the inherent bias becomes invisible. One such policy many colleges are moving towards, is continuous enrollment (Goldrick-Rab, 2006). These types of policies limit the reasons students may take a semester off, including financial reasons. Members of lower socioeconomic status (SES), who have significantly more financial constraints, are more likely to fail to meet this standard (Goldrick-Rab, 2006; Fomby, 2013). Although many attribute the lack of continuous enrollment by students in low SES populations to poor decision making, many of these students are making financially sound decisions to levy as little debt as possible. Developing policies that negatively impact students in lower SES populations disregards the value of economic diversity. Additionally, this policy has a concerning effect on Black STEM students especially considering STEM degrees are one of the costliest degrees to attain (Goldrick-Rab, 2006; Duncan & Magnuson, 2005). The combination of the impact institutionalized racism has on enrollment and retention leads to PWIs having significantly lower numbers of Black students than HBCUs. Thus, cultural stereotypes and the individualistic culture that exists at PWIs remains unchanged.

For the sake of this chapter and the focus on mentoring STEM majors, the rest of the discussion on institutionalized racism will focus on how this phenomena affects the retention rate of Black students in STEM majors. Black students progressing through the educational system often find themselves having to maneuver environments that are predicated in Eurocentric culture (Glocke, 2016). Researchers in this field believe that, at large, the educational system is designed to uplift White students at the expense of all others (Cornelius, 2014; Jackson, 2011). Glocke (2016) argues Black students struggle to learn in predominantly White schools because these institutions structure learning in a way that is not optimal for Black students. She states,

> the Eurocentric educational system utilizes: a universal and one size fits all approach; fosters competition; encourages rugged individualism and hierarchies; discourages class participation and interaction; is completely impersonal; emphasizes the memorization and regurgitation of information; believes that only one answer and one way of completing the work is correct; has no practical application; is devoid of critical thinking; demands perfection; and revolves around how quickly tasks and assignments are completed. (p. 107)

African/Black culture is built on foundations that controvert much of the assumptions of a Eurocentric educational system (Azibo, 2007; Myers, 1993). Therefore, it is no surprise that Black students often struggle to succeed in predominantly White schools.

In addition to a culture of Eurocentric education, institutionalized racism can impact Black STEM students in other ways. Researchers have noted, specifically for STEM programs, how masculinity in White culture may inhibit the experience and success of Black students (Flowers & Banda, 2015). STEM fields are still predominantly made up of White males and considered a masculine field of study (Flowers & Banda, 2015). Blacks often experience masculinity very differently than their White counterparts (Henfield, Moore, & Wood, 2008). While the masculine nature of STEM fields is an obvious hurdle for women, Carter (2005) postulates that Black males are often labeled as "non-compliant believers" because they fail to embrace the "feminization of acting white" (p. 49). The discrepancy between White masculinity and masculinity in other cultures can increase the problems Black students face in STEM programs and can lead to them being marginalized at PWIs (Smiler, 2004). This increase in problems and marginalization during their programs of study can lead Black students to change their majors. Now that a sketch of the different environments and the factors that impact the cultures at HBCUs and PWIs has been provided, we will take a look at how mentorships are enacted at these institutions.

Mentorship Across Institution Type

In general, successful mentorships for a variety of populations involve "career support, academic/research support and a personal relationship which include listening to concerns (emotional support) and problem solving" (Merriweather & Morgan, 2013, p. 2). Therefore, one might assume that mentoring at both institution types produces the same result for Black students. However, the picture is more complex than that. As the previous section illustrates, institutionalized racism produces a different environment at PWIs than at HBCUs for Black students. This environment can impact the success of Black students and how faculty interact with them (Nieto, 2010).

Who do you think I am? The dynamics of cross-cultural mentorships at PWIs. Due to the lack of availability of Black STEM faculty at PWIs (McCoy, Winkle-Wagner, & Luedke, 2015), there are times when White faculty end up mentoring Black students. These cross-cultural mentorships can be positive experiences, even still, Black students often recount the difficulty of these associations (Griffin, Perez, Holmes, & Mayo, 2010). While some Black students say they benefitted from having a White faculty mentor, they also speak to having felt like White faculty members did not expect as much from them as their White counterparts (Griffin et al., 2010). This decrease in expectation is partially due to some White faculty seeing Black students as Affirmative Action placements who did not get admitted based on their intelligence or competence (Brinson & Kottler, 1993; Merriweather & Morgan, 2013). This same phenomenon was shared in another study focused on colorblind mentoring (McCoy et al., 2015). When individuals believe that race does not matter, they are embracing colorblindness (Worthington, Navarro, Lowey, & Hart, 2008). A colorblind mentorship that refuses to accept inherent differences between White and Black students sets a precedent that those differences are unmentionable, and thus these differences are not given the needed attention and can be dehumanizing for the mentee. While there are a variety of negative facets to colorblind mentoring, one aspect focuses on viewing Black students as not being top students and providing them with extra allowances (McCoy et al., 2015). Viewed through Bonilla-Silva's (2010) colorblind racism frames, when White faculty perceive Black students in this way, they are naturalizing and totalizing. This means many White faculty *normalized* the idea that *all* Black students are less academically inclined. The consequence of this type of thinking is detrimental to the success of Black students in STEM programs. On one hand, Black students can come away from this type of mentorship espousing these same beliefs about themselves (McCoy et al., 2015). Thus, they run the risk of lowering their own expectations and career goals. On the other hand, White faculty may not encourage Black students to achieve at higher levels. This has the potential of limiting the growth trajectory and career goal attainment Black students at PWIs can achieve.

White faculty's lack of cultural competence can also serve to hinder the effectiveness of mentor relationships with Black students at PWIs (Merriweather & Morgan, 2013). White faculty often speak to how they treat Black students the same as all other students. This supposed standard treatment of all students serves to minimalize the culture and experiences of Black students (McCoy et al., 2015). When White faculty engage in colorblind mentoring, it can increase the potential for conflict between mentor and mentee. Conflict can happen because the mentor is not seeking to understand and attend to the lived experiences of Black students (Merriweather & Morgan, 2013). Further, White faculty may also have expectations that Black students assimilate into the culture of departments and the university (Winkle-Wagner & McCoy, 2016). As stated earlier, university and STEM departmental culture at PWIs is overwhelmingly Eurocentric. Therefore, expecting Black students to assimilate into this culture is next to asking them to abandon their own identities. This can

Different Worlds 71

lead to Black students having internal conflicts and a lower perseverance to complete academic programs (Winkle-Wagner, 2009).

In addition to a lack of cultural competence and seeing Black students as less academically capable, there can also be a power dynamic that serves to inhibit the effectiveness between White faculty and their Black mentees. All mentor relationships reside within the realm of a power differential (Crutcher, 2007). However, in mentorships between White faculty and Black students at Eurocentric institutions, White privilege is present. The presence of White privilege adds pressure to an existing power dynamic that already exists between mentor and mentee. If not acknowledged and discussed honestly, Black students can begin to feel talked down to. Researchers conceptualize this phenomena as paternalism (Jackman, 1994). Paternalism occurs when White faculty patronize Black students. Paternalism also serves to maintain the power structures that exist and reinforce stereotypes that Black students are academically underprepared (Jackman, 1994; McCoy et al., 2015).

There are challenges that can exist between White faculty at PWIs and their Black mentees. However, this does not mean these mentorships are not beneficial. The goal of this chapter is not to convince readers that White faculty cannot mentor Black students, but to highlight the context in which mentorships occur and speak to the dynamics of mentorships at PWIs and HBCUs. Given this goal, we will now turn to the dynamics of mentorships at HBCUs to see what lessons can be learned.

On the shoulders of giants: The dynamics of mentorships at HBCUs. In 2015, HBCUs accounted for 2% of all colleges, but conferred 17% of all bachelor's degrees to Black students—eight times the anticipated amount and nearly double their percentage of Black student enrollment rate (U.S. Department of Education, 2017). While this statistic cannot be solely attributed to the mentoring relationships at HBCUs, researchers have shown mentoring to be a critical factor in Black student success (McCoy, Winkle-Wagner, & Luedke, 2015). The mentoring experience of Black students majoring in STEM programs at HBCUs is different than the experience at PWIs. Some of this difference is attributed to Black students being able to have mentors they can identify with. However, the research is mixed regarding the true impact of this identity matching (Fries-Britt, Younger, & Hall, 2010). Nevertheless, describing the positive impacts of being able to identify with a mentor merits some attention. When Black STEM students at HBCUs are able to have a mentor that is also a member of an underrepresented population, this can serve to increase a mentee's self-efficacy. This increase in self-efficacy is due to a mentee seeing that he or she can achieve a desired set of goals because their mentor is proof of this possibility (Slovacek et al., 2011). In essence, having a mentor of like identity serves to reduce what Steele (1997) calls stereotype threat. Stereotype threat is,

> the event of a negative stereotype about a group to which one belongs becoming self-relevant, usually as a plausible interpretation for something one is doing, for an experience one is having, or for a situation one is in, that has relevance to one's self-definition. (Steele, 1997, p. 616)

Stereotype threat can cause Black students to internalize and begin to define themselves in light of negative stereotypes. In the case of Black STEM students, this could function to inhibit them from progressing forward in their career goals. Therefore, Black STEM students having a mentor they can identify with can help them contend with stereotypes held about their cultural group. This, in turn, functions to increase persistence in obtaining a STEM degree and career.

In addition to combatting stereotype threat, Black mentors also provide genuine psychological, academic, and career support. Many Black STEM faculty at HBCUs have already been through the system and had to struggle to overcome the negative stereotypes exhibited at PWIs. This experience allows these Black STEM mentors the ability to be empathetic to their Black STEM mentees and provide them with advice about maneuvering the Eurocentric field of STEM careers (McCoy et al., 2017). Further, Black STEM students speak about how they feel like their faculty at HBCUs really care about them and offer them research and professional opportunities (McCoy et al., 2017). In this way, Black STEM faculty at HBCUs function as social capital for their students and having access to this social capital is critical in obtaining jobs in STEM fields after graduation. In essence, the mentoring at HBCUs often takes on a life of its own, with Black faculty going above and beyond what is expected (i.e., other-mothering) to assist in the success of their mentees (McCoy et al., 2017).

As discussed earlier, the environment at HBCUs is familial and a place where other-mothering naturally occurs. Collins (2000) combined the concept of other-mothering with the education of Black students by stating, "Unlike the traditional mentoring so widely reported in the educational literature, this relationship goes far beyond that of providing students with either technical skills or a network of academic and professional contacts" (p. 191). Going far beyond includes a variety of practices and involves Black educators attending to Black students' emotional, psychological, economic, social, and political well-being (Foster, 1993; Guiffrida, 2005). African American mentors who engage in other-mothering have a comprehensive relationship with their students. These mentors provide career, academic and personal advising; support and advocacy; and a person who believes in a higher educational standard for Black students. This type of mentorship takes a lot work and time and while beneficial, these time-intensive mentor relationships have the potential for adverse impacts on Black STEM faculty.

Bearing an Unequal Load: The Impact of Mentorships on Black Faculty

In 2015, 15% of all college students were Black yet, 5% of all professors were Black (Education Department, 2018; U.S. Department of Education, National Center for Education Statistics, 2017). That accounts for a threefold decline in Black students who move past the college degree and into the professoriate in America. The discrepancy in Black professors and Black students was illustratively demonstrated by Strauss (2015) in *The Washington Post* article, "It's 2015. Where are all the black college faculty?" As Black students are followed throughout their academic careers, the percentages participating at each level drops significantly compared to White students, resulting in a dearth of Black professors at PWIs. Interestingly, the faculty composition at HBCUs has a different trend: approximately 60% of faculty are Black, 30% are White, and 10% are either Asian or Latino (Wei & Hendrix, 2016).

The racial composition of professors between PWIs and HBCUs has a significant impact on the mentoring outcomes of Black students. Black students report seeking out Black mentors (Griffin & Reddick, 2011). Being authentically sought out by a disproportionate percentage of the student body, Black professors will have a significantly larger mentor load than do their White colleagues at PWIs (Griffin & Reddick, 2011). The higher percentage of Black professors at HBCUs results in a more even spread of this mentorship load as there are more Black professors for Black students to seek out.

A larger mentorship burden can have adverse effects on a professor's ability to seek tenure at PWIs, as this limits the time that professors may spend engaging in activities valued by tenure committees, such as research (Golden, Bogan, Brown, Onwukwe, & Stewart, 2017). This devaluing by tenure committees of mentorship, which has been shown as a predictor of student success (Golden et al., 2017; Griffin, 2012), may be one more inadvertent policy that disproportionately affects the retention of Black STEM faculty at PWIs and thus Black STEM students.

PRESSING ON TOWARD
EFFECTIVE MENTORSHIPS AT ALL INSTITUTIONS

The picture painted of the differences in mentoring of Black STEM students at HBCUs versus PWIs might leave one wondering if Black students will ever more fully access STEM programs and career fields. There is good news. First, exploring the mentoring of Black students in STEM programs at HBCUs and PWIs provides lessons for how to move towards developing effective mentorships. Second, research shows that Black STEM students have experienced effective mentoring from White faculty in their programs at PWIs (Griffin et al., 2010). Therefore, it is not a question of whether White faculty can provide effective mentorships to Black STEM students. Rather, it is whether White STEM faculty will *choose* to attend to the lessons learned and serve as effective mentors to the Black students in their STEM programs. Below are a list of recommendations for how to improve mentor relationships between White STEM faculty and their Black mentees. While we have written the recommendations for White faculty, we acknowledge that not all Black faculty are proficient in mentoring Black STEM students. Remembering that Blacks are not a homogenous group (Palmer & Wood, 2012), there are Black STEM faculty who have different lived experiences than the students they mentor. With this in mind, Black STEM faculty who find themselves struggling to effectively mentor Black students can also find help in the recommendations below.

Recommendation 1: Increase Personal Awareness

This is a complex recommendation because there are many aspects of awareness White STEM faculty can have regarding their Black students. Admittedly, all aspects cannot be discussed here, but there are several to highlight from the discussion above. At the holistic level, White STEM faculty can increase their awareness of the systematic inequalities Black students face as they progress through the educational system (Feagin, 2014; Waymer & Street, 2016). A second aspect of awareness is learning about the culture of Black students and recognizing that the Eurocentric foundation of our education system can negatively impact the success of Black students in STEM programs (Glocke, 2016). A third, and more internal, aspect is for White STEM faculty to become aware of implicit biases they may have regarding Black students. Researchers have created assessments that provide information on the biases people hold regarding different people groups (see https://implicit.harvard.edu/implicit/). Taking assessments like these is merely a starting point for White faculty to engage in serious reflection about whether they hold negative stereotypes about Black students (McCoy et al., 2015). The final aspect to encourage awareness is admitting Black students are different from their peers in STEM programs. Engaging in colorblind mentoring is not beneficial but can actually serve to perpetuate racial stereotypes (McCoy et al., 2015). Pushing this further, White STEM faculty should remind themselves that Black students are not a homogenous group (Palmer & Wood, 2012) and come with a variety of experiences that necessitates individualized mentoring, just like their White counterparts. Becoming aware of these different aspects can serve to give White STEM faculty an understanding and appreciation for the road

Black students travel on their way to undergraduate and graduate STEM programs and should inspire them toward Recommendation 2.

Recommendation 2: Act on Your Awareness

Increasing one's awareness is a positive step forward, but acting on that awareness is what brings about change. As White STEM faculty increase their awareness of the aspects mentioned in Recommendation 1, they should allow themselves to mentor in different ways. White faculty should get to know their Black students in a deep way that allows Black students to feel cared for, heard and understood (i.e., other-mothering). These deeper mentor relationships provide mentoring that challenges and supports Black students and does not make allowances that serve to undermine student efficacy and persistence in STEM programs (McCoy et al., 2015). White faculty should be transparent and genuinely communicate their awareness of systematic inequalities and power dynamics inherent in the education system and their mentor relationship. This can serve to establish trust between White mentors and Black mentees (Merriweather & Morgan, 2013). White faculty should open their research labs to Black STEM students, so they can have experiences that will help them later in their STEM careers (McCoy et al., 2017). By engaging in these actions, White STEM faculty provide opportunities for Black STEM students to acquire social capital that can aid in future STEM career attainment (McCoy et al., 2017). Lastly, White STEM faculty should advocate for systematic changes in their program policies that currently reinforce White privilege.

Recommendation 3: Dust Yourself Off and Try Again

Learning to be an effective mentor to someone who is different from you takes work. White STEM faculty who want to be effective mentors to Black STEM students will likely make mistakes when attempting to engage their mentees. Overcoming a lifetime of biases and decades of racially-motivated policies is not easy. There may be times when White STEM faculty employ paternalism (Jackman, 1994) and engage in microaggressions against a Black STEM mentee. Occasions may arise when White STEM faculty revert to lowering their expectations of a STEM student they are mentoring, because the student is Black. When this happens, be aware of what is transpiring and why (Recommendation 1) and let that awareness motivate the engagement of more effective mentoring in future interactions with that student and other students (Recommendation 2).

SUMMARY

The number of STEM field job positions are steadily increasing and there is limited human capital to meet this demand (PCAST, 2012). Black populations provide a new pool to meet the growing demand for graduates in STEM fields. One of the focuses in attending to this demand is to increase diversity in STEM fields. Increasing diversity results in a wider array of perspectives for problem solving and idea development. Black populations also provide different perspectives due to the intrinsic difference in lived experiences than the current dominating Eurocentric perspective allows. The inclusion of diverse perspectives is important for problem solving since STEM fields are fairly homogenous (Flowers & Banda, 2015). If we are to expect a change in the culture surrounding STEM fields, there is a need for all institution types to produce diverse STEM graduates.

HBCUs graduate Black students at a much higher rate than PWIs (NCES, 2017; U.S. Department of Education, 2017). HBCUs exhibit a familial and high-energy culture (Glocke, 2016; Wei & Hendrix, 2016). PWIs are more Eurocentric and exhibit a more individualistic and competitive culture (Glocke, 2016). The culture at PWIs remains unchanged due to a lack of diverse student enrollment caused by phenomena, such as institutionalized racism (Jones, 2013). Further, the culture of PWIs, especially in STEM departments, is often centered around research. This research prioritization discourages faculty from undertaking a large mentoring load and encourages minimal involvement with mentees. This effectively fosters an environment that inhibits relationships which assist in the success of Black STEM students. We highlight how these cultural environments impact the mentoring that takes place at HBCUs and PWIs. The association between institutional culture and mentoring may help explain the higher graduation rates of Black students and more specifically Black STEM students at HBCUs.

Mentoring by Black faculty tends to be more hands-on and involved (Guiffrida, 2005). The Black mentors' concerns surpass that of academics and delve into the social realities of the students that may affect the academic success of Black STEM students. This mentor association is so involved that many have used the term other-mothering to describe it (Guiffrida, 2005). Mothers and children were often separated during the era of slavery. These children were raised by other adult female slaves and treated as if they were their own children. Other-mothers would ensure the children's needs were met and that they understood morals and ethics, just as their biological mother would have done (Collins, 2000; Dubey, 1995). Other-mothering has the added benefit of ensuring the mentor will develop a relationship with the mentee. When a relationship is formed, the mentor is aware of the strengths and challenges the Black student faces as well as the many facets that make their Black mentee unique.

Unfortunately, other-mothering is not the norm at PWIs. Black STEM students often feel as though the White faculty see them in a stereotypical and negative light (McCoy et al., 2015; Worthington et al., 2008). Researchers do use the familial term—paternalism—to describe the mentor relationship between White faculty and Black students. However, paternalism is not used in a positive light as this term speaks to Black students feeling as if the White faculty are condescending (Jackman, 1994). Further, White faculty at PWIs often do not seek to understand the lived experiences and culture of Black students. This lack of effort to understand Black students negatively impacts the quality of the mentor-mentee relationship, leaving Black students feeling as though they need to assimilate into White culture in order to succeed. The pressure to assimilate (spoken or unspoken) can negatively impact the retention and persistence of Black STEM students at PWIs (Merriweather & Morgan, 2013; Winkle-Wagner & McCoy, 2016).

Quality mentoring is important for the success of Black STEM students (Guiffrida, 2005). While there are differences that exist in mentoring between PWIs and HBCUs, the comparison between these two institution types gives rise to a variety of lessons for improving mentorships. Based on this information, we offer suggestions on how to improve the quality of mentoring at both institution types. We do this with the realization that regardless of institution type or ethnicity of the faculty member, there is always room for improvement, albeit in different ways. At the foundation of the lessons offered are the cyclical practices of reflection, awareness and action. If STEM faculty can engage in these practices, it may change the overall success of Black STEM students and as a result the place of the U.S. in the global STEM arena.

REFERENCES

Azibo, D. (2007). Articulating the distinction between Black Studies and the study of Blacks: The fundamental role of culture and the African-centered worldview (1992). In N. Norment, Jr. (Ed.), *The African American Studies reader* (2nd ed., pp. 525–546). Durham, NC: Carolina Academic Press.

Bonilla-Silva, E. (2010). *Racism without racist: Colorblind racism & radical inequality in contemporary American* (3rd ed.). Lanham, MD: Rowman & Littlefield.

Brinson, J., & Kottler, J. (1993). Cross-cultural mentoring in counselor education: A strategy for retaining minority faculty. *Counselor Education and Supervision, 32*(4), 241–254.

Carter, F. D., Mandell, M., & Maton, K. I. (2009). The influence of on-campus, academic year undergraduate research on STEM Ph.D. outcomes: Evidence from the Meyerhoff scholarship program. *Educational Evaluation and Policy Analysis, 31*(4), 441–462.

Carter, P. L. (2005). *'Keeping it real': School success beyond Black & White.* New York, NY: Oxford University Press.

Case, K. I. (1997). African American othermothering in the urban elementary school. *The Urban Review, 29*, 25–39.

Chen, P. D., Ingram, T. N., & Davis, L. K. (2014). Bridging student engagement and satisfaction: A comparison between historically Black colleges and universities and predominantly White institutions. *Journal of Negro Education, 83*, 565–579.

Collins, P. H. (2000). *Black feminist thought: Knowledge, consciousness, and the politics of empowerment.* New York, NY: Routledge.

Cornelius, C.D. (2014). *Afrocentric education: And its importance in African American children and youth development and academic excellence.* Charleston, NC: CreateSpace Independent Publishing Platform.

Crutcher, N. (2007). Mentoring across cultures. *The Education Digest, 73*(4), 21–25.

Dubey, M. (1995). Gayle Jones and the matrilineal metaphor of tradition. *Signs: Journal of Women in Culture and Society, 20*(2), 245–267.

Duncan, G. J., & Magnuson, K. A. (2005). Can family socioeconomic resources account for racial and ethnic test score gaps. *The Future of Children, 15*(1), 35–54. doi:10.1353/foc.2005.0004 ·

Education Department. (2018). Digest of education statistics 2016. Retrieved from http://books.google.com/books?id=mv6itAEACAAJ&hl=&source=gbs_api

Feagin, J. R. (2014). *Racist America: Roots, current realities, and future reparations.* New York, NY: Routledge,

Fries-Britt, S. L., Younger, T. K., & Hall, W. D. (2010). Lessons from high-achieving students of color in physics. *New Directions for Institutional Research, 2010*(148), 75–83. http://dx.doi.org/10.1002/ir.363

Flowers, A. M., III, & Banda, R. M. (2015). The masculinity paradox: Conceptualizing the experiences of men of color in STEM. *Culture, Society & Masculinities, 7*(1), 45–60.

Flowers, A. M., III, Scott, J. A., Riley, J. R., & Palmer, R. T. (2015). Beyond the call of duty: Building on othermothering for improving outcomes at historically black colleges and universities. *Journal of African American Males in Education, 6*(1). Retrieved from http://journalofafricanamericanmales.com/wp-content/uploads/2015/03/4Flowers2015.pdf

Fomby, P. (2013). Family instability and college enrollment and completion. *Population Research and Policy Review, 32*(4), 469–494. doi:10.1007/s11113-013-9284-7

Foster, M. (1993). Othermothers: Exploring the educational philosophy of Black American women teachers. In M. Arnot & K. Weiler (Eds.), *Feminism and social justice in education: International perspectives* (pp. 101–123). Washington, DC: Falmer Press.

Glocke, A. (2016). 'Round pegs into square holes:' Teaching black studies in an African centered way at predominantly white institutions. *Africology: The Journal of Pan African Studies, 9*(8), 102–134.

Goings, R. B. (2017). Traditional and nontraditional high-achieving black males' strategies for interacting with faculty at a historically black college and university. *The Journal of Men's Studies*, *25*(3), 316–335. Retrieved from http://journals.sagepub.com/doi/abs/10.1177/1060826517693388

Golden, A. A., Bogan, Y., Brown, L., Onwukwe, O., & Stewart, S. (2017). Faculty mentoring: Applying ecological theory to practice at historically black colleges or universities. *Journal of Human Behavior in the Social Environment*, *27*(5), 1–9. doi:10.1080/10911359.2017.1279097

Goldrick-Rab, S. (2006). Following their every move: An investigation of social-class differences in college pathways. *Sociology of Education*, *79*(1), 61–79.

Griffin, K. A. (2012). Black professors managing mentorship: Implications of applying social exchange frameworks to our understanding of the influence of student interaction on scholarly productivity. *Teachers College Record*, *114*(5), 1–37. Retrieved from https://works.bepress.com/kimberly_griffin/22/download

Griffin, K. A., Perez, D., II, Holmes, A. P. E., & Mayo, C. E. P. (2010). Investing in the future: The importance of faculty in development of students of color in STEM. *New Directions for Institutional Research*, *2010*(148), 95–103. http://dx.doi.org/10.1002/ir.365

Griffin, K. A., & Reddick, R. J. (2011). Surveillance and sacrifice. *American Educational Research Journal*, *48*(5), 1032–1057. doi:10.3102/0002831211405025

Guiffrida, D. (2005). Othermothering as a framework for understanding African American students' definitions of student-centered faculty. *The Journal of Higher Education*, *76*(6), 701–723.

Henfield, M. S., Moore, J. L., & Wood, C. (2008). Inside and outside gifted education programming: Hidden challenges for African American students. *Exceptional Children*, *74*(4), 433–450.

Hernandez, P. R., Schultz, P., Estrada, M., Woodcock, A., & Chance, R. C. (2013). Sustaining optimal motivation: A longitudinal analysis of interventions to broaden participation of underrepresented students in STEM. *Journal of Educational Psychology*, *105*, 89–107.

Hill, O. W., Pettus, W. C., & Hedin, B. A. (1990). Three studies of factors affecting the attitudes of blacks and females toward the pursuit of science and science-related careers. *Journal of Research in Science Teaching*, *27*(4), 289–314.

Jackman, M. R. (1994). *Velvet glove: Paternalism and conflict in gender, class, and race relations*. Berkeley, CA: University of California Press.

Jackson, Y. (2011). *The pedagogy of confidence: Inspiring high intellectual performance in urban schools*. New York, NY: Teachers College Press.

Jones, W. A. (2013). Prestige among black colleges: Examining the predictors of HBCU peer academic reputation. *Journal of African American Studies*, *17*(2), 129–141. doi:10.2307/43525451

Kamara, M. (2007). Are us news' rankings inherently biased against black colleges. *Diverse Issues in Higher Education*, *24*(10), 8. Retrieved from http://search.proquest.com/openview/2af6c8bea76ad34da2d3cff28119af19/1?pq-origsite=gscholar&cbl=27805

McCoy, D. L., Courtney, L. L., & Winkle-Wagner, R. (2017). Encouraged or weeded out: Perspectives of students of color in the STEM disciplines on faculty interactions. *Journal of College Student Development, 58*(5), 657–673. https://doi.org/10.1353/csd.2017.0052

McCoy, D.L., Winkle-Wagner, R., & Luedke, C.L. (2015). Colorblind mentor? Exploring White faculty mentoring of students of color. *Journal of Diversity in Higher Education, 8*(4), 225–242.

Merriweather, L. R., & Morgan, A. J. (2013). Two cultures collide: Bridging the generation gap in a non-traditional mentorship. *The Qualitative Report, 18*(12), 1–16. http://www.nova.edu/ssss/QR/QR18/merriweather12.pdf

Myers, C. B., & Pavel, D. M. (2011). Underrepresented students in stem: The transition from undergraduate to graduate programs. *Journal of Diversity in Higher Education, 4*(2), 90–105. doi:10.1037/a0021679

Myers, L.J. (1993). *Understanding an Afrocentric world view: Introduction to optimal psychology.* Dubuque, IA: Kendall/Hunt.

National Science Foundation (NSF). (2003). *Women, minorities, and person with disabilities in science and engineering, 2002.* Arlington, VA: Author.

Nieto, S. (2010). *Language, culture, and teaching: Critical perspectives for a new century* (2nd ed.). New York, NY: Routledge.

Palmer, R. T., & Wood, J. L. (2012). Black men in college. Retrieved from https://play.google.com/store/books/details?id=G-rFBQAAQBAJ&source=gbs_api

Perkins, L. (1989). The history of Blacks in teaching: Growth and decline with the profession. In D. Warren (Ed.), *American teachers: Histories of a profession at work* (pp. 344–369). New York, NY: American Educational Research Association.

Peterfreund, A. R., Rath, K. A., Xenos, S. P., & Bayliss, F. (2008). The impact of supplemental instruction on students in STEM courses: Results from San Francisco State University. *Journal of College Student Retention, 9*(4), 487–503.

President's Council of Advisors on Science and Technology (PCAST). (2014). *Engage to excel: Producing one million additional college graduates with degrees in STEM.* Washington, DC: Author.

Smiler, A. (2004). Thirty years after the discovery of gender: Psychological concepts and measures of masculinity. *Sex Roles, 50,* 15–26.

Slovacek, S. P., Whittinghill, J. C., Tucker, S., Peterfreund, A. R., Rath, K. A., Kuehn, G. D., & Reinke, Y. G. (2011). Minority students severely underrepresented in science, technology engineering and math. *Journal of STEM Education. 12,* 5–16.

Steele, C. M. (1997). A threat in the air. *American Psychologist, 52*(6), 613–629.

Stewart, P. (2004). Who's playin' whom. *Diverse Issues in Higher Education, 21*(5), 26. Retrieved from http://search.proquest.com/openview/ffae5e0f1cadc690f00ab a30c6f0a3db/1?pq-origsite=gscholar&cbl=27805

Strauss, V. (2015). It's 2015. Where are all the Black college faculty. *The Washington Post.* Retrieved from https://www.washingtonpost.com/news/answer-sheet/wp/2015/11/12/its-2015-where-are-all-the-black-college-faculty/

Tillman, L. C. (2001) Mentoring African American faculty in predominantly white institutions. *Research in Higher Education, 42*(2), 295–325.

U.S. Department of Education, National Center for Education Statistics. (2016). Digest of education statistics, 2015 (NCES 2016-014). Retrieved from https://nces.ed.gov/pubsearch/pubsinfo.asp?pubid=2016014

U.S. Department of Education, National Center for Education Statistics. (2017). Integrated Postsecondary Education Data System (IPEDS), "Fall Enrollment Survey" (IPEDS-EF:90) IPEDS Spring 2001, Spring 2011, and Spring 2017, Fall Enrollment component; IPEDS Spring 2017, Finance component; and IPEDS Fall 2016, Completions component. Retrieved from https://files.eric.ed.gov/fulltext/ED486443.pdf

Waymer, D., & Street, J. (2016). Second-class, cash strapped, antiquated institutions: Unbalanced media depictions of historically black colleges and universities in the chronicle of higher education. *Journal of Multicultural Education, 10*(4), 489–506.

Wei, F.-Y. F., & Hendrix, K. G. (2016). Minority and majority faculty members in a historically black college/university: Redefining professors' teacher credibility and classroom management. *Qualitative Research Reports in Communication, 17*(1), 102–111. doi:10.1080/17459435.2016.1220419

Winkle-Wagner, R., & McCoy, D. L. (2016). Entering the (postgraduate) field: Underrepresented students' acquisition of cultural and social capital in graduate school preparation programs. *Journal of Higher Education, 87*(2), 178–205.

Winkle-Wagner, R. (2009). *The unchosen me: Race, gender, and identity among Black women in college.* Baltimore, MD: Johns Hopkins University Press.

Worthington, R. L., Navarro, R. L., Lowey, M., & Hart, J. (2008). Color-blind racial attitudes, social dominance orientation, racial-ethnic group membership and college students' perceptions of campus climate. *Journal of Diversity in Higher Education, 1,* 8–19. http://dx.doi.org/10.1037/1938-8926.1.1.8

CHAPTER 5

STEM DOCTORAL STUDENT DEGREE ATTAINMENT

How Demands, Structures, and Networks Impact Timely Degree Completion

Carrie Klein
George Mason University

Hironao Okahana
Council of Graduate Schools

INTRODUCTION

In the past decade, there has been a concerted effort to diversify doctoral student pools and to increase timely student completion of doctoral degrees in science, engineering, technology, and mathematics (STEM) fields. According to the National Science Foundation (NSF), only 6.5% of those who earned research doctorates in STEM fields in 2016 from U.S. degree granting institutions were students of traditionally underrepresented minority (URM) backgrounds as defined by the NSF (2018a) to

---

Seeing The HiddEn Minority, pp. 83–98
Copyright © 2020 by Information Age Publishing
All rights of reproduction in any form reserved.

include, Hispanic or Latino, American Indian or Alaska Native, or Black or African American persons. Although, this is an improvement from a decade ago, URM students continue to be underrepresented in STEM doctoral education. Further, there is evidence to suggest that URM student paths may look different from those of White and Asian counterparts. For those URM students who do complete, their path to completion in some STEM fields appears to take longer than their White and Asian counterparts (NSF, 2018b). Median time-to-doctorate since entering doctoral programs for Hispanic or Latino, American Indian or Alaska Native, or Black or African American students are close to those of their White and Asian counterparts in most STEM broad fields; however, median time-to-doctorate since entering graduate school, as well as since earning their bachelor's degrees, are longer for URM students in almost all broad STEM fields (NSF, 2018b). Furthermore, a study of URM STEM doctoral students at 21 U.S. research universities found that having prior master's degrees positively correlated with likelihood of degree completion among Black/African American students, as well as URM men (Okahana, Klein, Allum, & Sowell, 2018). This suggests that URM student pathways may not be a continuous transition from bachelor to doctoral degrees.

This lack of representation and longer time to completion is problematic, as the strength of the U.S. national economy, including its workforce and global competitiveness, is tied to its diversity and to degrees and career pathways that are "available to all Americans" (National Science Board [NSB], 2014, p. 22; Council of Graduate Schools, 2007). There is also a personal cost to students who choose not to or who take longer to complete, as current and future income and opportunities that require advanced degrees may not be accessible to them or will take longer to realize. Thus, facilitating the timely degree completion of a more inclusive and diverse STEM doctoral workforce is an issue of importance on multiple fronts.

However, what timely degree completions means is often ill-defined. Timely degree completion is viewed as an important outcome measure of success for doctoral programs. Higher education institutions are often focused on timely degree completion for all students as a means of communicating organizational success in an environment that is increasingly focused on institutional transparency and accountability (Hearn, 2015). The discussion of broadening participation of URM students in STEM fields, has placed an emphasis on achieving higher STEM doctoral completion rates among URM students with shorter time-to-degree. However, whether or not any benchmarks for *timeliness* (e.g., six-year completion rates, eight-year completion rates, etc.) are reflective of timely degree completion is unclear, because there is no clear definition of what timely completion of STEM doctoral degrees means and studies considering completion rates vary broadly (Spittle, 2013).

Further, the notion of timeliness, itself, is a manifestation of one-size-fit all approach in guiding and mentoring URM students through STEM doctoral experience. It negates the contexts and realities of URM doctoral students experiences. It does not account for timeliness from the perspectives of students, nor does it take into account the various organizational structures, including policies and support, that may be impacting *timely* completion rates. Additionally, extant research has often focused on a deficit model, in which various student variables, rather than embedded structural issues of doctoral programs, are seen as attributing to longer degree completion rates (Rendón, Jalomo, & Nora, 2000).

Given the complexities of timely degree completion, it is important to understand what individual and institutional factors contribute to time-to-degree for URM doctoral students. Through interviews with former doctoral students who successfully completed their degrees, we investigated their perspectives on their programs and their experiences to understand how those programs and experiences informed their time-to-degree. The findings from this study provide insight into how individual demands, institutional structures, and networks of support can influence degree completion timeliness. This chapter also proposes a reconceptualization about how we speak about timeliness toward STEM doctoral completion, based on these insights.

CONTEXT OF THE STUDY

To gain a more complete picture of student experiences related to timely degree completion, we used an interactive qualitative research design per Maxwell (2008). This approach allowed us to "harmoniously" (p. 215) connect our methods with existing literature on URM doctoral student experiences, findings from an overarching research project focused on URM doctoral student attrition and completion, and the goals of our inquiry.

This study was part of a larger research project conducted by the Council of Graduate Schools (CGS) and supported by the NSF (Grant No. 1131884). The larger project investigated the attrition and completion rates of URM doctoral students in STEM programs at 21 universities within the United States. The overall project, which is the largest study of its kind to use graduate student-level data, unearthed the various factors influencing attrition, completion, and time-to-degree of STEM URM doctoral students.

Among the findings of the overall project were that URM doctoral student experiences are as unique as the students themselves, yet most students shared feelings related to the intensity, solitude, and complexity of doctoral education (Sowell, Allum, & Okahana, 2015). Other findings included insights into institutional structures and policies as being barriers or promoters to student attrition or completion, and the importance of advisor, mentor, and peer relationships. Participants also noted the importance of programs that aim to increase the number of URM students in STEM fields, like the NSF Alliances for Graduate Education and the Professoriate (AGEP) (Sowell, Allum, & Okahana, 2015). These programs appear to address funding concerns and create opportunities for socialization and peer support (Sowell, Allum, & Okahana, 2015). Although the overall project sheds light on factors that influence attrition and completion of URM students in STEM doctoral programs, these insights were derived only from current doctoral students. Data included in this chapter is from additional interviews that were conducted with degree completers to shed further light on the institutional and personal factors contributed their successful completion of their doctorates and their time-to-degree completion.

In this smaller study, we used data from interviews with ten URM doctoral degree recipients in STEM fields from public research universities in a southeastern state in the United States. Through contact with deans of graduate schools of four public research universities that had participated in the larger research project, URM students, who began and earned their STEM doctoral degrees between July 1992 and June 2012, were recruited to participate in the interviews. We chose to focus on one particular state in this study because: (1) the four institutions made up the largest number of institutions in a single state from the larger, overarching research project, and (2) none of the institutions had NSF AGEP support. This way, the experience of URM doctoral degree holders were somewhat similar geographically and institutionally. In total, 10 URM STEM doctoral degree recipients agreed to participate in the interviews. All 10 earned their doctorates in social and behavioral sciences fields.

Prior to interviewing participants, we obtained IRB approval. Telephone interviews lasted approximately an hour each, and, through semi-structured interviews, we asked participants about their experiences as doctoral students. Interview questions focused on the reasons students pursued doctoral degrees, the various academic and nonacademic demands on student time, the support systems and structures available to students, and any existing barriers that delayed their progress to degree. Examples of questions asked included: (a) Why did you decide to pursue a doctoral degree; (b) What aspects, if any, of your program were demanding?; (c) Did you have any major life events occur during your program?; (d) What

STEM Doctoral Student Degree Attainment   87

sort of relationship did you have with your advisor?; (e) What role did peers play in your progress?; and (f) What other program or institutional factors promoted or constrained your degree progress. Interviews were audio recorded and transcribed. We systematically coded the transcripts to analyze the data. Codes were created based on both a review of the literature and theory related to doctoral degree completion, URM degree pathways, and URM student academic experiences, and as they emerged through our analysis. Additional codes were added that emerged from the data. Example codes included: barriers, incentives, infrastructures, resources, demands, and support. From those codes, among others, we derived the themes that guide the following section of the chapter.

Emerging Themes of Doctoral Experience

Themes that emerged from this inquiry and are presented in this chapter confirm much of what is already known to improve student engagement, retention, and completion. Namely, that doctoral students face multiple demands on their time (e.g., financial and familial) that can impact time-to-degree and that institutional funding, advising, peer mentoring, and institutional structures are important factors that also influence time-to-degree. However, this study brings new insight into individual and institutional factors related to URM doctoral degree completion and areas for further research. Specifically, themes related to attempts to balance competing demands (which often resulted in juggling, not balance), structural impacts of institutions and their programs (including funding, policies, and outreach) and having networks of support (inclusive of formal and informal faculty, other experts, and peers). Implications and areas for further research that emerged from this study include understanding that longer time-to-degree is not always a negative from the student perspective; that color-blind institutional policies and mentoring and support practices may hinder, rather than promote, student progress and success; and that the importance of URM doctoral students having networks of support to encourage completion, regardless of their timeline, toward doctorates is a vital component for degree completion. What follows is an exploration of the themes that emerged from this inquiry and the extant literature that informed both the development and understanding of those themes. The chapter concludes with implications and recommendations for future research and practice, based on the findings from our inquiry.

Juggling Outside Demands. For the URM doctoral recipients we interviewed, finding a balance between academic and nonacademic demands is challenging and creates significant environmental pulls on their time. Doctoral students from all backgrounds typically enter their programs with individual responsibilities (e.g., work responsibilities and family demands), within the context of their academic programs (e.g., level of financial support, socialization, and campus climate). These factors can influence the time it takes to complete a degree (Ehrenberg & Mavros, 1995; Gardner, 2008; Golde, 1998, 2000, & 2005; Kim & Otts, 2010; Maher, Ford, & Thompson, 2004; Seagram, Gould, & Pyke 1998; Zhou & Okahana, 2016). Study participants argued that doctoral-level course work was often challenging, but not overly so. For example, one noted in an interview, "Classes were difficult, but you knew they were going to be difficult—that's why you were going to school." However, it was the impact of other demands outside of being doctoral students, including work, parenthood, and major life events, that created the greatest challenge for participants.

All of the participants interviewed noted that it was often impossible to find balance between the demands of their academic coursework and the demands outside of their program. Rather, they just made their situations work by juggling the various demands in their lives, which required a high-degree of organization, motivation, and planning on their parts. A participant explained the complexities of her situation during graduate school, "There were financial needs for my family, so I worked full time, tried to be a full-time student, and work on my dissertation. That really took a lot." Alternatively, when they could, participants put off major life events, as one former student explained, "I purposefully made the decision to postpone child rearing and bearing until later." While participants acknowledged that this juggling impacted their time-to-degree, they also stated that juggling of this nature is unavoidable.

Of the people we interviewed, most were full time students during their doctoral programs with some sort of financial support from their institutions that at least partially covered their tuition and fees. Most of such support was a result of working as a teaching or research assistant. Two of the participants (including one part-time student) held full-time jobs that remitted tuition costs. Participants noted the importance of having additional income during their doctoral program to help cover living expenses or care for family members, as funding from their programs was not enough to cover their needs. One participant noted, "Of course, I had to pay my bills, so that made [the program] stressful in addition to coursework." Despite the need to work, these students were also often advised by their faculty or advisors not to work, so that they could focus completely on completing their degree. Another noted, "My professors always warned us against working." For most participants, this was unrealistic or unwanted advice, as they viewed work as not just a necessity, but also often as an opportunity. Students had similar thoughts about attending to family responsibilities—those responsibilities were not just needed, but a wanted part of their experiences. Advice by program faculty or advisors to limit outside responsibilities created tensions for participants in our study.

Attempts to juggle competing demands often resulted in longer time-to-degree, even when those outside demands were deemed positive in nature. One student noted that she obtained her dream job prior to starting her dissertation. While this ultimately delayed her progress, she not only eventually finished her degree, but has moved up the ranks in the company that hired her during graduate school. Another student got married and had a child, events that he said he did not regret even though it made completing his degree more challenging. He reflected, "My professor thought I was crazy to have a kid, crazy to get married. I think there was an expectation from some of them that you should just sort of live at the lab ... to be here 24-7, and I couldn't do that." For this participant, having a life in addition to a degree was of value, even if it took him longer to earn that degree.

Institutions and graduate programs value timely degree completion as studies have shown that students are more likely to complete when less time is spent on the doctoral degree (Kim & Otts, 2010). However, in this inquiry participants repeatedly stated that, while they could have finished faster with better funding, less outside work, and fewer family obligations, they did not view the longer time-to-degree as problematic. To them other competing priorities were equally as important and enriching for their lives as earning a doctoral degree. Moreover, participants often wanted their programs and institutions to recognize such experiences that happen outside of, but were related to, their degree progress, like employment in their field. While this finding is likely not unique to URM students, it does suggest a potential disconnect between how institutions and students view timely degree completion and its import. This disconnect may be universal and experienced by students from all backgrounds, but could also be rooted in the issue of modern students interacting with traditional academic structures and policies.

Structural Impacts. Students are juggling multiple demands within normative and gendered academic structures that were designed for and are primarily inhabited by a professoriate and administrative staff that does not necessarily look like them and who have not had similar graduate school experiences (Acker, 2012; Lester, Sallee, & Hart, 2017). In 2013, only 3.8% of all doctoral faculty members in Science and Engineering fields were Black/African American. Similarly, 4.3% and 0.2% respectively were Hispanic/Latino S&E doctoral faculty members and American Indian/Alaska Native faculty members (NSF, 2014). Further, many faculty members—as many as 92% of tenured science and engineering (S&E) doctoral faculty members, who account for 75% of all tenured or tenure-track faculty members in S&E fields in 2013—earned their doctorates more than a decade ago. Thus, many of the tenured faculty members who are advising URM students are likely to have completed graduate training during a time with greater levels of graduate student funding (NSF, n.d.) and within normative structures that were in alignment with their identity (Lester, Sallee, & Hart, 2017). For URM doctoral students navigating increasingly costly graduate education within the normative structures of higher education can be difficult. As such URM doctoral students are often interacting with structures, policies, and advising related to degree completion that do not conform with their realities or perspectives. These structures, policies, and advising practices assume a one-size-fits all model of graduate study, often not taking into account the unique experiences of individuals within the current context of higher education. One participant shared an example of how policies and student realities related to assumptions around time and funding often do not align and lead to difficult decisions for students:

> Some Ph.D. students have saving or family to support them, but the enrollment process, the way courses are set up, you set up your courses on Monday and by Friday you have to pay your tuition, otherwise you get a late fee. And the response [from the department chair] was "Oh well, just put it on your credit card." And so, that happens to a lot of students, students who may not have the resources to put something [like tuition] on a credit card until the next pay day.

This payment policy puts students in a difficult financial situation, which can impact their degree progress, and does not recognize the reality of student who may, given the financial realities of graduate education, may not have the financial flexibility to charge their tuition to a credit card. Rigid policies with tight timelines, especially associated with financial issues can delay student progression. While this example is specific to this participant and her specific institution, it is representative of a broader issue of structural impediments that may delay degree progression and completion.

Moreover, as another participant argued, while well-intentioned, the creation and use of depersonalized policies and advising by institutions, programs, and faculty creates an environment in which students of color may not feel fully comfortable or integrated into their programs. She noted that she loved her program and completed her degree in a timely fashion, but that her university:

> Really doesn't acknowledge that minority students are minority. I wasn't discriminated against, but I wasn't acknowledged either. You aren't going to offend minority students because you acknowledge their background. Don't treat them differently, but acknowledge them. I felt like the program was color blind ... but a color acceptance model might be a better fit for minority students.

When students are not acknowledged for who they are, when they do not feel a sense of belonging or feel that they are working in structures that are creating unnecessary or uninformed barriers to their progress, they are more likely to feel othered and to disengage. Creating an environment in which doctoral students are welcome, integrated, and supported for who they are, at multiple levels, are important factors related to doctoral completion (Gardner, 2008; Golde, 1998, 2000, & 2005; Maher, Ford, & Thompson, 2004; Seagram, Gould, & Pyke 1998; Zhou & Okahana, 2016).

However, the use of color-blind (i.e., race-neutral) policies to provide that support is seen by students in our study as problematic. Increasingly, color-blind policies are being understood as "an ultramodern or contemporary form of racism and legitimizing ideology used to justify the racial status quo" (Bonilla-Silva, 2009; Harper, 2012; Neville, Awad, Flores, & Bluemel, 2013, p. 455). As a result, color-blind policies often work to further the normalize embedded and dominant structures in social institutions, like education, that can further marginalize and oppress URM students (Crenshaw, Gotanda, Peller, & Thomas, 1995; Delgado & Stefancic, 2000; Harper & Hurtado, 2007; Williams & Land, 2006). Blanket policies and interactions related to degree completion, like measuring aggregated time-to-degree, that do not account for individual or racial minority student perspectives, may hinder URM doctoral student experiences and degree progress.

While structural barriers to integration and support existed for participants, a few reported that their programs worked well to reach across those barriers to create positive and supportive environments, by reaching out to them before their programs began and by continuing to support them, as individuals and as members of a community, throughout their programs of study. These sentiments are somewhat corroborated by lukewarm approval of how well STEM programs and faculty members are doing to address issues facing URM students (Sowell, Allum, & Okahana, 2015). In a survey of 1,640 URM STEM doctoral students, 31% agreed or strongly agreed that faculty members are aware of issues facing URM students, while 26% disagreed or strongly disagreed (Sowell, Allum, & Okahana, 2015). This is an area in which STEM programs can do better. Participants from programs that worked to personalize their experience noted greater satisfaction with their programs, overall. Based on conversations with these former students, having institutionalized and personalized support as a part of a broader network of support is a key component to student success and timely degree completion. Prior work has acknowledged the importance of departmental support in time-to-degree rates for students, and this study was no exception (Maher, Ford, & Thompson, 2004; Seagram, Gould, & Pyke 1998; Zhou & Okahana, 2016).

Networks of Support. Key to successful degree completion, at all levels, by URM students in STEM fields are faculty -student interactions and relationships. Numerous studies have underscored the importance of faculty-student interactions at the undergraduate level in improving URM student retention and completion in STEM fields (Cole, 2010; Eagan, Hurtado, & Chang, 2010; Hurtado, Eagan, Tran, Newman, Chang, & Velasco, 2013; Kim & Sax, 2009), and evidence from extant literature has also noted importance of mentoring in promoting student success in graduate education (Brown, Davis, & McClendon, 1999; Creighton, Creighton, & Parks, 2010; Crisp & Cruz, 2009; Rose, 2005; Thomas, Willis, & Davis, 2007). This correlation continues at the doctoral level, specifically, as faculty interactions, especially mentors, provide feedback, encouragement, and practical advice that can help students complete their degrees in a timely manner (Curtin, Malley, & Stewart, 2015, p. 714; Gardner & Barnes, 2014).

However, an important theme to emerge from this inquiry is the importance for URM doctoral students to have not just support or interactions from an individual faculty member or mentor, but rather to have a network of supportive faculty mentors. Sorcinelli and Yun (2007), in their discussion of faculty mentoring, describe support networks as being a "flexible network of support in which no single person is expected to possess the expertise required to help someone navigate the shoals of a faculty career" (p. 58). Based on the conversations with doctoral recipients in this study, the benefits of support networks extend to doctoral student development, as they allow students to access members of their networks, throughout their academic careers, to address specific needs or interests.

The participants we interviewed noted that their networks were typically composed of academic program advisors or mentors (advisors were often, but not always, viewed as mentors), external mentors (who were often faculty from other departments or disciplines or were individuals outside of academia), peers (who ranged from classmates to peer advisors), and family or community members. Moreover, participants stated that these networks were composed of both formally constructed relationships through the university or program's structures (e.g., assignment of a major advisor or incoming peer cohort orientations and events), but also evolved organically through individual relationship building between students and their faculty and peers. These networks of support can also play a role in augmenting support that students may otherwise seek from faculty advisers. One participant explained how she cultivated a network of support, "My advisor knew the program requirements and was on top of things. I was grateful, because even though [the relationship] wasn't the best fit, I was able to get a lot of other support from other faculty."

Proper fit of mentors was often cited by participants as an important component of their support in their programs and often spurred them to seek out other mentors, resulting in a network of support. The advantage of having a network of support was that it provided students with guidance from a variety of informed and supportive sources that helped move them forward in their program, even when a main advising faculty member is a poor or an incomplete fit as a mentor. Although some participants noted that assigned advisors were not always supportive beyond basic advising, many noted that their advisors also acted as mentors. One participant noted the difference: "An advisor gives you advice on which way to go, but a mentor actually shows you how to navigate the system and shows you how to live life." Types of mentoring were different and tailored to the specific needs of each of the participants, providing them support that varied from course advising, to career development, to administrative problem solving. Having someone, either within or outside of their program that acted, not just as an advisor, but also as a mentor was vital to participants' timely completion.

The advantages of mentoring relationships in keeping students on track and moving forward toward graduation extended to peer interactions both social and academic in nature, like writing or dissertation groups. Participants noted time and again how both formal and informal relationships with peers helped keep them motivated. One participant noted that her support network was a blend of official departmental advising and of a "quasi-official departmental group," a coursework group, and a dissertation group. Particularly important for participants were structured relationships that were established early and maintained over the course of the doctoral program. For instance, prior to starting her program, one participant was paired with a more senior member of the program, who acted as her formal mentor throughout the course of study, even after that peer mentor had left the program. Another participant, through the work of her faculty advisor, participated in weekly meetings with fellow students to explore faculty work, help each other with conference proposals and presentations, and prepare for dissertation defenses. Another participant, whose program provided less structured support for students, created a study and writing group with friends, the basis of which was to keep peers motivated and celebrate their successes. The existence of support networks is an important element for successful and timely doctoral degree completion for URM students.

Implications, Recommendations, and Future Work

The rich descriptions by our participants of their doctoral student experiences illustrate the demands and experiences that URM STEM doctoral students navigate in their programs. These competing demands, which often come from family and outside work obligations, appear often to be in conflict with normative and gendered structures of the academy. These conflicts are not necessary explicit or intentional; however, their existence calls for sensitivity by administration and faculty members in advising and guiding URM graduate students through STEM doctoral programs and in considering and working to minimize the impacts of embedded organizational structures, dominant discourses, and marginalizing policies on these students. Further, time-to-degree can be shortened or prolonged via the types of structures, policies, and support networks students encounter during their doctoral studies. Based on these emergent findings and related literature, there are important implications for graduate program administrators and for future research.

First, the existence of support networks, not just individual advisors or mentors, are vital to student completion. Aspects of these networks should be facilitated, when possible, by graduate programs, so that support does not only exist organically in pockets of graduate programs, but also is embedded in all aspects of graduate program structures. Most importantly, the faculty and administrative members who are a part of these networks should receive professional development and training on how to provide supportive and personalized advising to their students based on who their students are, as individuals and as URM students, not on normed or color-blind institutional perspectives of who, as students, they should be.

This professional development training will likely require a rethinking of structures and policies that exist that may limit student's timely progression. As a part of this rethinking, programs should consider advising approaches and assessment of time-to-degree. Given the importance of fit for advisor/student relationships, programs that do not explicitly layout the process of advisor changes may want to adopt a model wherein students are assigned an initial advisor with an understanding, by all parties, that advising partnerships may changes as a student progresses through their program. Moreover, mentoring should be conceptualized as an ongoing relationship focused on the totality of the student experience, not just on dissertation research and degree completion. Ongoing, annual check-ins, portfolio reviews, or use of individual development plans by committees or mentoring networks should be institutionally encouraged.

Also, an important implication to emerge from this study is the disconnect between student perspectives on timely degree completion. From the student and institutional perspective, a longer time to completion may be perceived as a positive, especially when it means time for marriage, the birth of a child, or time to care for a family member. However, taking a semester off to tend to life events is often counted against a student's completion time for assessment and reporting purposes. Akin to stopping the tenure clock for tenure-track assistant professors, programs may want to reassess time-to-degree measures to account for major life events.

Finally, the desire for students to be seen as individuals and for their experiences as people of color to matter and to be acknowledged in program policies and in advising and mentoring interactions is important to encourage. This important finding, one that promotes a color acceptance versus color blind model of interaction, needs further research and recommendations for practice specific to URM doctoral student experiences. Acknowledging the varied lived experiences of people of color in graduate school programs may improve feelings of integration, which could, in turn, improve time-to-degree rates and to student experiences and support. Most importantly, this work is vital as a means to problematize long-held assumptions and practices that are embedded in higher education institutions related to time-to-degree and student experiences. More work needs to be done in this area to fully understand what factors can be leveraged to support URM doctoral students move through their program toward degree completion at a pace that works for them and for their institutions.

CONCLUSION

Findings that emerged from these interviews include the roles that competing demands, structural impacts, and mentoring networks have on timely student degree completion. We link these findings to a number of recommendations. Specifically, the need for doctoral processes to incorporate elements of negotiation between students and their advisors—and creating a structural environment that facilitates such negotiation—emerged from these findings. This process should include an understanding of students as individuals with unique experiences, needs, and aspirations, as well as an understanding that competing priorities, particularly family and outside work obligations, do not necessarily make students less committed to pursuing a doctorate than those without such obligations. Further, doctoral programs intentional creation and communication of program policies and practices that can help facilitate successful completion through equitable, but individualized support. Finally, programs should help URM students craft a network of supportive faculty, administrators, and staff to help them navigate and successfully complete their programs.

ACKNOWLEDGMENTS

This chapter is based upon work supported by the National Science Foundation under Grant No. 1138814. Any opinions, findings, and conclusions or recommendations expressed in this article are those of the authors and do not necessarily reflect the views of the National Science Foundation or the Council of Graduate Schools.

REFERENCES

Acker, J. (2012). Gendered organizations and intersectionality: Problems and possibilities. *Equality, Diversity and Inclusion: An International Journal, 31*(3), 214–224.

Bonilla-Silva, E. (2009). *Racism without racists: Colorblind racism and the persistence of racial inequality in the United States* (3rd ed.). Lanham, MD: Rowman & Littlefield.

Brown, M. C., II, Davis, G. L., & McClendon, S. A. (1999). Mentoring graduate students of color: Myths, models, and modes. *Peabody Journal of Education, 74*(2), 105–118.

Creighton, L., Creighton, T., & Parks, D. (2010). Mentoring to degree completion: Expanding the horizons of doctoral protégés. *Mentoring & Tutoring: Partnership in Learning, 18*(1), 39–52.

Crisp, G., & Cruz, I. (2009). Mentoring college students: A critical review of the literature between 1990 and 2007. *Research in Higher Education, 50*(6), 525–545.

Cole, D. (2010). The effects of student-faculty interactions on minority students' college grades: Differences between aggregated and disaggregated data. *Journal of the Professoriate, 3*(2), 137–160.

Council of Graduate Schools. (2007). *Graduate education: The backbone of American competitiveness and innovation*. Washington, DC: Author.

Crenshaw, K., Gotanda, N., Peller, G., & Thomas, K. (1995). *Critical race theory: The key writings that formed the movement*. New York, NY: The New Press.

Curtin, N., Malley, J., & Stewart, A. J. (2016). Mentoring the next generation of faculty: Supporting academic career aspirations among doctoral students. *Research in Higher Education, 57*(6), 714–738.

Delgado, R., & Stefancic, J. (Eds.). (2000). *Critical race theory: The cutting edge*. Philadelphia, PA: Temple University Press.

Eagan, M. K., Hurtado, S., & Chang, M. J. (2010, October). *What matters in STEM: Institutional contexts that influence STEM bachelor's degree completion rates*. Paper presented at the Annual Meeting of the Association for the Study of Higher Education, Indianapolis, IN.

Ehrenberg, R., G., & Mavros, P. G. (1995). Do doctoral students' financial support patterns affect their times-to-degree and completion probabilities? *Journal of Human Resources, 30*(3), 581–609.

Gardner, S. K. (2008). Fitting the mold of graduate school: A qualitative study of socialization in doctoral education. *Innovative Higher Education, 33*(2), 125–138.

Gardner, S. K., & Barnes, B. J. (2014). Advising and mentoring doctoral students: A handbook. *Faculty and Staff Monograph Publications. 210.* CreateSpace Independent Publishing Platform. Retrieved from https://digitalcommons.library.umaine.edu/fac_monographs/210

Golde, C. M. (1998). Beginning graduate school: Explaining first-year doctoral attrition. *New Directions for Higher Education, 1998*(101), 55–64.

Golde, C. M. (2000). Should I stay or should I go? Student descriptions of the doctoral attrition process. *The Review of Higher Education, 23*(2), 199–227.

Golde, C. M. (2005). The role of the department and discipline in doctoral student attrition: Lessons from four departments. *The Journal of Higher Education, 76*(6), 669–700.

Harper, S. R. (2012). Race without racism: How higher education researchers minimize racist institutional norms. *The Review of Higher Education, 36*(1), 9–29.

Harper, S. R., & Hurtado, S. (2007). Nine themes in campus racial climates and implications for institutional transformation. *New Directions for Student Services, 2007*(120), 7–24.

Hearn, J. C. (2015). *Outcomes-based funding in historical and comparative contexts.* A Lumina Issue Paper prepared for HCM Strategists. Indianapolis, IN: Lumina Foundation.

Hurtado, S., Eagan, M. K., Tran, M. C., Newman, C. B., Chang, M. J., & Velasco, P. (2011). "We do science here": Underrepresented students' interactions with faculty in different college contexts. *Journal of Social Issues, 67*(3), 553–579.

Kim, D., & Otts, C. (2010). The effect of loans on time to doctorate degree: Differences by race/ethnicity, field of study, and institutional characteristics. *The Journal of Higher Education, 81*(1), 1–32.

Kim, Y. K., & Sax, L. J. (2009). Student-faculty interaction in research universities: Differences by student gender, race, social class, and first-generation status. *Research in Higher Education, 50*, 37–459. doi:10.1007/s11162-009-9127-x

Lester, J., Sallee, M., & Hart, J. (2017). Beyond gendered universities? Implications for research on gender in organizations. *NASPA Journal About Women in Higher Education, 10*(1), 1–26.

Maher, M. A., Ford, M. E., & Thompson, C. M. (2004). Degree progress of women doctoral students: Factors that constrain, facilitate, and differentiate. *The Review of Higher Education, 27*(3), 385–408.

Maxwell, J. (2008). Designing a qualitative research study. In L. Bickman & D. J. Rog (Eds.), *The SAGE handbook of applied social research methods* (pp. 214–252). Thousand Oaks, CA: SAGE.

National Science Board. 2014. Science and Engineering Indicators 2014. Arlington VA: National Science Foundation (NSB 14-01).

National Science Foundation. (n.d.). WebCASPAR, Integrated Science and Engineering Resources Data System. Retrieved from https://ncsesdata.nsf.gov/webcaspar/

National Science Foundation. (2014). Survey of Doctorate Recipients, 2013 (Public Use Data File). Retrieved from https://ncsesdata.nsf.gov/datadownload/

National Science Foundation. (2018a). Table 22. Doctorate recipients, by subfield of study, citizenship status, ethnicity, and race: 2016. In 2016 Doctoral Recipients from U.S. Universities. Retrieved from https://www.nsf.gov/statistics/2018/nsf18304/datatables/tab22.htm

National Science Foundation. (2018b). Table 32. Median years to doctorate, by sex, citizenship status, ethnicity, race, and broad field of study: 2016. In 2016 Doctoral Recipients from U.S. Universities. Retrieved from https://www.nsf.gov/statistics/2018/nsf18304/datatables/tab32.htm

Neville, H. A., Awad, G. H., Brooks, J. E., Flores, M. P., & Bluemel, J. (2013). Color-blind racial ideology: Theory, training, and measurement implications in psychology. *American Psychologist*, *68*(6), 455.

Okahana, H., Klein, C., Allum, J., & Sowell, R. (2018). STEM Doctoral completion of underrepresented minority students: Challenges and opportunities for improving participation in the doctoral workforce. *Innovative Higher Education*, *4*(43), 237–255. https://doi.org/10.1007/s10755-018-9425-3

Rendón, L. I., Jalomo, R. E., & Nora, A. (2000). Theoretical considerations in the study of minority student retention in higher education. *Reworking the Student Departure Puzzle*, *1*, 127–156.

Rose, G. L. (2005). group differences in graduate students' concepts of the ideal mentor. *Research in Higher Education*, *46*(1), 53–80.

Seagram, B. C., Gould, J., & Pyke, S. W. (1998). An investigation of gender and other variables on time to completion of doctoral degrees. *Research in Higher Education*, *39*(3), 319–335.

Sorcinelli, M. D., & Yun, J. (2007). From mentor to mentoring networks: Mentoring in the new academy. *Change: The Magazine of Higher Learning*, *39*(6), 58–61.

Sowell, R., Allum, J., & Okahana, H. (2015). *Doctoral initiative on minority attrition and completion*. Washington, DC: Council of Graduate Schools.

Spittle, B. (2013). Reframing retention strategy: A focus on progress. *New Directions for Higher Education*, *2013*(161), 27–37.

Thomas, K. M., Willis, L. A., & Davis, J. (2007). Mentoring minority graduate students: Issues and strategies for institutions, faculty, and students. *Equal Opportunities International*, *26*(3), 178–192.

Williams, D. G., & Land, R. R. (2006). Special focus: The legitimation of Black subordination: The impact of color-blind ideology on African American education. *The Journal of Negro Education*, *75*(4), 579–588.

Zhou, E., & Okahana, H. (2016). The role of department supports on doctoral completion and time-to-degree. *Journal of College Student Retention: Research, Theory & Practice*, Advance online publication. doi:10.1177/1521025116682036

SECTION III

IDENTITY

CHAPTER 6

THE ROLE OF IDENTITY ON PERSISTENCE FOR BLACK WOMEN DOCTORAL STUDENTS IN SCIENCE

Andrea L. Tyler
Tennessee State University

Letimicia Fears
Vanderbilt University

Monica L. Miles
Cornell University

BLACK WOMEN IN SCIENCE

It is well documented that African Americans are underrepresented in the sciences at the undergraduate and graduate levels (Jett, 2019; Morton & Parsons, 2018). Historically, Black students pursuing science, technology, engineering, and math (STEM) degrees have faced the typical challenges associated with pursuing a STEM degree, as well as the challenges related

Seeing The HiddEn Minority, pp. 101–120
Copyright © 2020 by Information Age Publishing
All rights of reproduction in any form reserved.

to stereotypes that influence how others view them (McGee & Bentley, 2017). Racial stereotypes have communicated to Blacks in STEM fields that they are not intellectually qualified to pursue degrees and or careers in STEM. Despite their consistent effort and achievements, Black students in STEM doubt their competence and future success in the STEM fields (McGee & Bentley, 2017). African American science students are likely to experience racial microaggressions (Dortch & Patel, 2017), though they deal with racial battle fatigue (Pierce, 1995) and stereotype threat (Beasley & Fischer, 2012). African American students in college attribute the positive influence of parents, high expectations placed on them by family and school and precollege experiences and curriculum as themes for success (Russell & Atwater, 2005). Gifted and advanced education is often a precollege curriculum.

Despite racially hostile environments, the number of underrepresented minority women earning graduate degrees has more than doubled in the last 20 years (National Center for Science and Engineering Statistics [NCSES], 2017). The proportion of Black women with early-career doctorates is higher than their male counterparts (NCSES, 2017). Black women also report their physical and social activities and self-worth are all impacted by being in graduate school (Longfield, Romas, & Irwin, 2006). The lack of socialization and the constant question of the competence of Black women in STEM education led some to be proactive in preventing damage to their self-image (Joseph, 2012). Although they experienced neglect, isolation, and discrimination regularly, Black women reported that they did not internalize those experiences. Instead, they remained committed to their goals of pursuing a degree in the STEM fields (Joseph, 2012).

IDENTITY AND SCIENCE

We understand identity to be self-assigned categories or descriptions that we use to help us relate to the world around us. Identity is not a fixed entity; identity develops as life events, as well as biological and psychological changes that occur (Kroger, 2015). According to Bertrand Jones, Wilder, and Osborne-Lampkin (2013), multiple identities, including race and gender, that exist for Black women intersect in ways that need acknowledgment during the socialization process and continued persistence in STEM. Black women hold a duplicitous identity that is trapped in systemic and structural inequalities that racialized and gendered beings face in a White patriarchal society (Tyler & Muhammed, 2014).

STEM fields have a reputation for being male dominated, but in recent years more women have begun to pursue education and careers in those areas. While there has been a slight increase in the number of women in

STEM fields, Black women remain grossly underrepresented (Morton, 2020). Despite the increase of Black women, they represent approximately 25% of students enrolled in graduate programs in STEM (Allum & Okahana, 2015). Researchers have discussed various factors that serve as contributors to the lack of Black women. Those factors mainly include gender and racial differences and a lack of resources available to Black women in the fields (Beoku-Betts, 2004). Historically, Black women have been viewed as incompetent and inferior to their male counterparts in the science fields (Joseph, 2012).

Common stereotypes in STEM fields assume that Black people, in general, are less competent than their White counterparts and that women do not belong in science careers (Charleston, Adserias, Lang, & Jackson, 2014). The well-documented and well-known stereotypes about Black women in society at large penetrate and follow these women into their science spaces (Charleston et al., 2014; Morton & Parsons, 2018), which can cause them to fear being labeled as "the angry black woman, lazy, or unintelligent" (Joseph, 2012; McGee & Bentley, 2017). Due to repetitive attacks of their intelligence, low expectations, and isolation from faculty and peers, Black women in science reported having a lack of self-confidence and belief in their abilities. While these experiences may deter Black women from entering STEM fields upon graduating, these complexities contribute to challenges in forming one's identity and legitimacy as a Black woman scientist in academia (Brewer, 1999). The limitations in access and preparedness, research suggests that the United States educational system's continuous disengagement, undereducation, and underutilization of women of color at all levels of academia is systemically problematic and continues to perpetuate marginalization (Charleston et al., 2014; Farinde & Lewis, 2012; Johnson, Brown, Carlone, & Cuevas, 2011; Syed & Chemers, 2011).

Research on girls' self-efficacy in math and science subjects shows a startling reality: girls begin experiencing gender stereotypes of STEM subjects as early as elementary school (Stratton, n.d.). This stereotype bias and marginalized efforts are especially true among Black girls (Haynes & Joseph, 2016). For example, early childhood girls of color are socialized to believe that they are inadequate in math and science subjects and subsequently self-select out due to a lack of early, engaging experiences (Brickhouse, Lowery, & Shultz, 2000; Stratton, n.d.). The amalgamation of various factors, such as gender stereotypes, pedagogical techniques, and STEM curricula, unwittingly deter young women from developing and maintaining interest in STEM fields, as well as developing a STEM identity (Brickhouse et al., 2000). Also, students of color may not be given or are significantly limited in their access to STEM courses, computers, and other technical information (Bullock 2017; Charleston et al., 2014). It is also the case that the aforementioned factors that impact academic marginalization (both intentional and unintentional) inherently contribute to Black women being left out of opportunities to develop further their skills necessary to be successful in STEM.

Not only is the environment in which a person experiences and engages with STEM critical in helping foster a STEM identity, but the perception of resources and support (both tangible and intangible) aid in the formation of a STEM identity (Carlone & Johnson, 2007; Lee, 2002; Merolla & Serpe, 2013; Merolla, Serpe, Stryker, & Schultz, 2012).

BLACK WOMEN, IDENTITY, AND PERSISTENCE

Researchers have recognized that Black girls are lost in the leaky STEM pipeline in early education, resulting in a wealth of literature around the science identity and achievement of African American girls in science classrooms (Joseph, Hailu, & Boston, 2017). Low achievement of minority students has been blamed on socialization and discrimination (McGee & Bentley, 2017) and inferior cognitive abilities (Hernstein & Murray, 1994), but more recent studies combat these assertions. For example, Thompson (2014) reported that African American girls that were failing their science classes were able to improve their grades and understanding of science when the science was made open for critique, and they were able to develop personal narratives to the science. Another such example is early gifted education, Black girls that participate in gifted education outperform their counterparts without access to gifted education in mathematics and science (Wright, Ford, & Young, 2017).

The development of a science identity is strongly linked to the continued pursuit of science for Black girls and women in STEM. Carlone and Johnson (2007) describe science identity as "how women make meaning in science and how social structures those possible meanings." It is essential for Black girls to be able to identify with the science to maintain engagement. The typical science classroom offers a few limited science identities (Carlone & Johnson, 2007) with few opportunities to engage in identity-related conversation to make the science more relatable (Huber, Whelan, & Clandinin, 2003). Even high achieving minority students struggle to identify with science careers (Wong, 2012), suggesting that the women that achieve high degrees and careers in science have constructed their own identities to help them persevere and or are not coping well. There is evidence to support both of those possibilities; Black women employ parental and peer

The Role of Identity 105

support (Breakwell & Beardsell, 1992) as well as faculty mentors to help them reach their postcollege goals (Morales, 2008). As graduate students, Black women feel a definite sense of self-worth associated with success in academics (Morton, 2020) but also suffer from an elation/depression cycle and delayed gratification in graduate school (Longfield et al., 2006).

THEORETICAL FRAMEWORKS

Within the vast epistemological assumptions are two theoretical frameworks that guide the data collection and analysis processes. These frameworks were used to explore the multiple identities of three Black women pursuing doctoral degrees in science. These identities simultaneously exist within and are affected by systems of privilege and power within the social context of science education. Two frameworks, *the multiple dimensions of identity model* (Jones & McEwen, 2000) (Figure 6.1) and *Black feminist thought* (Collin, 1991), were used to situate the identities into a broader context. These frameworks serve as a foundation for understanding the multiple and complex identities. The purpose of using this conjoined approach in analyzing the lives of Black women is as a means of illustrating the effects of how the dominant narrative, which delegitimizes the existence of the Black women in STEM doctoral programs, marginalized and disenfranchised Black women. Moreover, this approach must focus on these women's experiences to capture and understand their varied, unique, and nuanced experiences of being Black and female in the science field.

Multiple Dimensions of Identity

The model of multiple dimensions of identity (Jones & McEwen, 2000) underscores the importance of acknowledging an individual's multiple identities, the intersections of these identities, and how social and academic contextual factors influence the development of these identity dimensions. Additionally, Black feminist thought (Collins, 2000) is used to inform the reader and analyze the results of the research by placing women and their experiences at the core of the analyses. Additionally, this theoretical framework explores, examines, and evaluates the voices and experiences of Black women as one which characterizes a uniformity of specific shared experiences, yet individualized and nonspecific in other respects (Osmond & Thorne, 1993). Listening and conceptualizing the nuanced voices of single, Black women is critical to closing the void that currently exists about the lived experiences of this subgroup of women (Price, 1996).

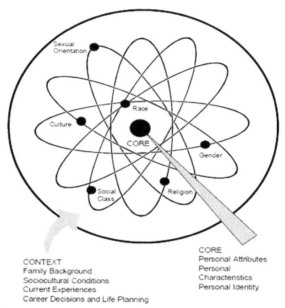

Source: Jones and McEwen (2000).

Figure 6.1. Model of multiple dimensions of identity.

Black Feminist Thought

Black feminist thought (Collins, 2000) is the second theoretical framework that grounds this study. The Black feminist thought lens is used to inform the reader and to analyze the results by placing Black women and their experiences at the core of the analyses. Additionally, this theoretical framework explores, examines, and evaluates the voices and experiences of the Black women as one which characterizes a uniformity of specific shared experiences, yet individualized and nonspecific in other respects (Osmond & Thorne, 1993). Listening and conceptualizing the nuanced voices of Black women is critical to closing the gap that currently exists about the lived experiences of this subgroup of women in general (Price, 1996) and in the science field specifically (Morton, 2020). The scholarship of Black feminist thought, and knowledge reproduction collides head-on with the inherent "othering" and opposed thought of the dominant narrative in science education (Tyler & Muhammed, 2014).

The purpose of this research was to explore Black women graduate students' perception of their identities and how the intersection of these identity constructs may influence their persistence in a science doctoral program. Two research questions guided the study:

1. *How do Black women in a science doctoral program position and negotiate their identities?*
2. *How are Black women using their identities to help them persist through their science doctoral programs?*

METHODOLOGY

The chapter highlights the empirical work that investigates how the participants conceptualize the notion of prescribed identities and persistence. A qualitative approach was used due to the dearth of research about graduate education at HBCUs. By employing a qualitative approach to examine multiple identities and socialization, the researcher acknowledges the social structures inherent in STEM disciplines (Davis, 2008). The qualitative methodology also allows for the identification of unanticipated phenomena and influences (Maxwell, 1996) and facilitates a better understanding of what was primarily an exploratory study (Creswell, 2003).

As a qualitative inquiry, a phenomenological methodology was utilized in the discovery and understanding of their lived experiences of three Black women in science and how their lived experiences motivated them to persist. Phenomenological research is where the researcher reveals "the essence of human experiences about a phenomenon as described by participants" (Creswell, 2009, p. 12). A phenomenological point of view takes into consideration the concept that human behavior is a result of a specific incident or phenomenon, rather than an occurrence that is objective or external to the individual experiencing the event (Sloan & Bowe, 2014).

Participants

The participants in this study are three Black women that attended a public institution located in the Southeastern region of the United States. Walker University, a pseudonym, is classified as a midsize historically Black colleges and university (HBCU). HBCUs have a longstanding history of being the largest producers of Black graduates in science. Despite this history, the demographics have been transitioning to where Black students are a numerical minority among students and faculty in STEM (Ortiz, Morton, Miles, & Roby, 2020). Which positioned the three Black women in a context where their race and gender minoritize them. The researchers identified three doctoral fellows, two in biological sciences and one in physical therapy, ranging in age from 22 to 30, and they all self-identify as Black women. The study participants also served as university doctoral fellows and were exposed to behavioral and psychological tenets, such as

108   A. L. TYLER, L. FEARS, and M. L. MILES

identity, socialization, and persistence in STEM. The three participants were a part of the same cohort, thus building a sense of community among themselves. Participation in this study was voluntary, and a pseudonym was given to each participant to protect their identity (see Table 6.1).

The researchers chose purposeful sampling to select the participants for this in-depth study (Patton, 1990). This type of sampling is selected for cases that are "information-rich and illuminative; that is, they offer useful manifestations of the phenomenon of interest" (Patton, 2002, p. 40). Criteria for sampling included (1) graduate college students who attended Walker University at the time of the study; (2) self-identify as Black women; (3) majoring in a science discipline; and (4) participating in the same program cohort.

Table 6.1.
Research Study Participants

Name (pseudonyms)	Classification	University (pseudonym)	Major
Mo'Nique	Second-year doctoral student	Walker University	Biological Sciences
Lisa	Third-year doctoral student	Walker University	Physical Therapy
Tonya	Fourth-year doctoral student	Walker University	Biological Sciences

Data Collection

A study consent form was e-mailed to the selected participant describing the purpose of the study and the study expectations. The consent form described the current and future use of the data collected, their rights as participants, and how their confidentiality and anonymity would be protected. Involvement in the study was voluntary; however, all three participants consented to participate in the study via written consent. Data collection consists of an interview, a focus group, and generalized written narratives.

Interviews

Data was collected from each participant through an in-depth semistructured interview that served as the primary source of data collection and allowed for in-depth questioning (Kvale & Brinkmann,

2009). The interview questions were open-ended and designed to elicit the individual stories of each participant (Lieblich, Tuval-Mashiach, & Zilber, 1998) and provided insight into the women's experiences at their university campus and within their science departments. The semistructured interviews lasted 30 to 45 minutes, and Dedoose software was used to transcribe each interview. All interviews were audiotapes and transcribed verbatim. Follow-up questions were asked of each participant to clarify the participants' responses (Colaizzi, 1978) and to encourage complete and detailed account of their experiences while attempting not to influence any of their responses (Englander, 2010; Giogo, 2009). The second author conducted the interviews via Skype and the telephone.

A second session was held as a form of member checking to ensure the researchers captured the essence of their experiences. Member checking allowed participants to make corrections, where necessary, and ensure data accuracy. Each participant was sent their transcribed interview via e-mail, and they validated the integrity of the data by written approval.

Journal Prompts

In addition to the interviews, written narratives, using open-ended questions, were collected to assess better and supplement the interviews. Strauss (1987) called these additional documents "slices of data," which allow "for further coding, including the discovery of relationships among the various categories that are entering into emergent theory" (p. 27). These additional resources aid in confirming or denying commonalities observed throughout the data. Since it was aimed to understand persistence and experiences and distinguish some characteristics through the lens of identity, persistence, degree attainment, and career trajectory.

Data Analysis

Each interview and focus group was transcribed verbatim for each participant to identify salient patterns supported by the text. Analysis of the semistructured interview data followed a three-step coding process. First, the interviews were read through two times to identify the flow and pattern of each participant's interview and the relationship to articulating their lived experiences of identity and feminist thinking. Second, each interview was color-coded, and themes were identified and organized into larger thematic themes that were common to each participant. Each narrative testimony was organized to reflect the pattern of how each participant articulated their interpretation of identity, persistence, and Black women in science in the third step of the analysis. After analyzing the interviews, the focus group and generalized written narrative data were analyzed using the same logic as the interviews.

The researchers used open coding (Strauss & Corbin, 1990) to analyze the interviews and the focus group session. Open coding entailed reviewing the interview transcripts line-by-line and focusing on the actual words of the participants, followed by the thematic organization of the codes using an Excel spreadsheet. The words were then grouped together into concepts that represented the same phenomena. The concepts applied were related to the underlined themes of the study and the ways in which the participants moved toward identity and feminist understanding of Black women in the sciences. The coding architecture for the data analysis allowed for the identification of unanticipated phenomena and influences (Maxwell, 1996) and facilitated a better understanding of the study (Creswell, 2003). The data were uploaded to a secure website where the files were stored via encrypted and password-protected computer files to protect the confidentiality of the participants.

In conclusion, the researchers used two theoretical frameworks that complemented the study design and allowed the researchers to understand the meanings the participants made of their multiple identities. Narrative inquiry, as the research methodology, enabled the researchers to ask broad interview questions that encouraged the participants to discuss in-depth how they perceived their identities. This methodological approach than provided them the opportunity to analyze and generously reconstruct the participants' stories into both individual and encompassing narratives that attempt to portray the richness of their Black identities in science.

Positionality Statement

Collectively as Black women in STEM, we were able to detect the nuances about Black culture and experiences and determine the interconnection of identity and science in higher education. It is, therefore, important that we discuss the aspects of our identity and reflect on how our identities shape this study.

Andrea—I received my degrees in engineering and educational leadership, with a focus on science and engineering education. I completed my degrees at a HBCU and a predominately White institution (PWI). As a Black female engineer, I feel as if this research epitomizes who I am as a teacher and a social science researcher. My research focuses on the experiences of Blacks in STEM, especially Black women, and how we must negotiate the multiple identities that exist within us. This research is personal to me, and as I continue to interrogate the dominant discourse that continues to perpetuate that Black girls/women do not succeed in STEM narrative.

The Role of Identity   111

Letimicia—I received my undergraduate and master's degree in biology, and my doctoral degrees in biological sciences. I completed my degrees at a PWI and a HBCU. I currently work as a K–12 science educator and program evaluator in a large urban school district. These experiences have helped me develop my passion for science education, in general, but more specifically with girls and students of color.

Monica—I have a background in science, and I am a P–20 social science researcher with a focus on STEM education. I completed all my degrees at PWIs, which allowed me to be more sensitive to the distinctions between HBCUs and PWIs (Ridgeway, 2019).

FINDINGS

The purpose of this chapter is to discuss the findings in relation to the research questions and the theoretical frameworks that guided this study. The purpose of this study was to examine ways in which Black women doctoral students majoring in science persist while managing multiple identities at a HBCU. The two research questions that guided this study are: (1) How do Black women in a science doctoral program position and negotiate their identities? (2) How are Black women using their identities to help them persist through their science doctoral programs?

Despite previous research that speaks to the disparity of Black women students in science fields (Farinde & Lewis, 2012), this research takes the approach of looking through a positive orientation that described common identity dimensions among the three participants and how they described these identities as sources of support. Findings suggest the following thematic categories across all the women to be impactful to their persistence and success in science: family and friends, religion and spirituality, and self-care and fitness identity.

The Complexities of Black Women's Identity in Science

All of the women within the study self-identified as being Black women. All three participants described how both their race and gender identities were interconnected. When the women were queried about the interconnectedness about their race-gendered identities, they all responded that there were other aspects of their identities that were equally as salient in science. The women's complex explanations of their salient identities challenge the current intersectionality research practices, which often will engage race and gender, and very few studies explore beyond these two dimensions.

The women were all well aware of the racist and sexist environments in which they are navigating in the larger society and within science. Tonya stated, "I expect to experience racism for being black and misogyny for being a woman.... And White men are the majority members of the STEM area." Like many Black women in science, Tonya's sentiments highlight the isolation the women experienced in tandem with racist and sexist climates. Mo'Nique added, "I see myself as an outcast. Most of the time I feel like I'm outside the scientific community wise. I feel like I'm still a watcher." This isolation and exclusion from the scientific community reify how science spaces can be toxic for women, even at an HBCU. Even at HBCUs, Black women are minoritized, and Blacks students overall have become the numerical minority in STEM. Which can explain why the women feel isolated within their programs.

The women recognized that they were hypervisible in science spaces, but this was not always a negative perception. Mo'Nique described how her hypervisibility could serve as a representation for other Black youth to join science because they see her. Overall the women positively responded to how they drew on sources of support to thrive and persist in science. This discovery is perhaps why many of the women leveraged other parts of their identities to resist these structures and cope. For example, when Lisa responded to what her most salient identities within science, she responded, "I would say, my family, my spirituality, my education, and my drive to achieve at life." Lisa later elaborates to describe these aspects of her identity are important because they are sources of support to continue to persist. Lisa finished this list with " my drive to achieve at life," while intrinsic motivation has been identified as an important characteristic in persistence, it is also the least that she described. Lisa heavily relies on and values her family and church community outside of science to make sense of her experiences and her desire to persist.

Family and Friends: A Social Identity

All of the women described the various ways their family supported them in their journey, from providing specific career advice to wanting to be a role model because they were the first. Mo'Nique shared how she is "one of the first [in her family], and they don't really understand" which causes her family to ask her many questions about her program and her experience. "You know I've gotten support from them. It is definitely hard or difficult for them to understand and identify with me." While Mo'Nique's family does not have the institutional knowledge of higher education, they value

The Role of Identity 113

her choices, and she still finds her interactions with them supportive. On the other hand, Lisa and Tonya describe their families and have been able to provide specific career advice, which helps them navigate. Tonya shared, "My immediate family has always given me advice on my career. My family has been very supportive of me, as well." Lisa shares how her family is:

> involved in my academic career because I still live at home…. They are definitely there for me and are great support…guiding me to my next steps. My mother is a leader in a prominent community organization, so she definitely has connections to people in the medical field that have opened doors for me."

While Mo'Nique's family does not have the connections or the career advice to aid her in navigating the science field, she receives this support from her HBCU. Mo'Nique stated:

> Ever since coming to [Walker University] I have developed more of a bond as far as personal bonds because faculty are people too. I've met some of the faculty members' children, and … if they see me, they would recognize me…. This has helped me with retention [in the program] because I have been through a couple of deaths while being at [Walker University] and the support has helped me a lot … instead of just dropping out because of course you don't have your own family here they made it easier for me.

Providing students with familial or kin-folk connections is impactful for Black students' persistence and retention in higher education programs.

Fulfilling My Destiny: A Religion and Spiritual Identity

All three women described themselves as primarily spiritual and feeling as if they were living their life's purpose because of their beliefs. Furthermore, while they did not have the same religious background, they described how their spiritual practice enabled them to persist. For example, Mo'Nique described how she was raised as a "Traditional Christian" but today identifies more as spiritual and "takes from Hinduism, Buddhism, Gnosticism, Judaism, etc." Lisa added, "It's [spirituality] definitely is one of my foundations that keeps me sane in this crazy world, and it helps me get through. Prayer definitely helps me get through school and the challenges I have had." The Black community has traditionally relied on spirituality as a source of encouragement through trying times, and these Black women are continuing that practice through their pursuits in higher education.

Maintaining Their Temple: A Self-Care and Fitness Identity

While physical fitness is important to overall health and wellbeing, all of the women described the role that physical fitness has played in persisting in their programs from running to yoga and being in boot camps they participated in outside of their institution. Tonya shared, " I eat healthier and workout, but in undergrad, I did not exercise much at all." Lisa continued with "[working out] has really been helping me relieve stress from the job and giving me an outlet." Mo'Nique shared, " outside of school that [working out] helped me cope … I think it was actually a major factor that kept me motivated and going … I feel good after it." These women use physical activity as a way to reduce stress, increase self-esteem, and boost their mood and increase their cognitive functions.

This study described data collected from three Black women pursuing their doctoral degrees in science. Black women graduate students perceive their multiple identities and social connectedness as a major part of their persistence in doctoral science programs. The findings were consistent with all three women and showed that the participant's surroundings, considered in connection with inherent race and gender identities, constructed their multiple dimensions of identities and a sense of self. Specifically, the participant's view of the findings shows that identity dimensions such as religion and spirituality, family and friends, and fitness and self-care are salient and contribute to their persistence in science.

DISCUSSION/CONCLUSION

This study aimed to increase the body of knowledge about Black women in science and their persistence in graduate school. In this section, the researchers discuss the study findings, the research questions, and the theoretical frameworks that guided this study. The purpose of this study was to examine ways in which Black women doctoral students majoring in science persist while managing multiple identities at a HBCUs. The two research questions that guided this study are: (1) How do Black women in a science doctoral program position and negotiate their identities? (2) How are Black women using their identities to help them persist through their science doctoral programs? The results of the study indicated that the two research questions are interconnected. The researchers, therefore, discuss them in conjunction with one another.

The participants in the study spoke about race and gender as salient dimensions of identity; however, the findings from the study revealed new identities that collectively made a well-rounded person. The new identity of several of the participants made meaning of their existence in the graduate

The Role of Identity   115

science programs. According to Bertrand-Jones et al. (2013), multiple identities, including race and gender, that exist for Black women intersect in ways that need acknowledgment during their matriculation. In addition to the underlying inherent identities, the present study revealed that these women expressed the need for spirituality, physical fitness, and familial relationships to encourage their persistence in science doctoral programs.

The participants described and made meaning of their identities in multiple ways. For the participants identifying as Black women were a source of liberation and strength; an identity that brought them confidence and a feeling of being centered. However, identifying as a Black female in a science field at sometimes could be misinterpreted as a source of hardship or discrimination, translated into either a painful existence or false empowered. When all five identities were intertwined and seen as equal, the perception of what it meant to be Black in the sciences was revealed, in some respect, allowing them [the participants] to become whole.

In general, the participants found the appropriate dimensions into which the identity fit. The multiple identities helped them understand themselves by providing a ready-made identity or a sense of connection to family, friends, community, and religion. Some participants were less interested in labels but were not prepared to abandon these, either because they had worked so hard at understanding the meaning of their identity or considered them necessary means of existence.

Despite the many successes attributed to the graduate experience in helping to retain Black women in science disciplines, Black students still have the highest STEM attrition rate among all other populations (Chen, 2013). Research question two calls for the investigation of how persistence and identities relate to Black women in science; while uncovering the perception, understanding, and influence of their race, gender, family, and religious identities.

In investigating their experiences from a multiple identity perspective, this study provides several insights on science persistence. These insights may be useful for graduate education experiences and science education researchers. First, this study finds Black women draw strength and empowerment from their race and gender identities, where if they can make a personal connection between their identity and science, they would be likely to associate identity and persistence in science. Each participant has lived experiences rooted in several overlapping identities and social constructs; for example, gender, race, social, age, community, and family composition. The convergence of these identities and constructs contribute to the epistemologies used in persistence and educational attainment.

Black women should not have to navigate racially hostile science spaces alone. This study aimed to show how these science spaces can learn from the Black women and the sources of support needed to foster strong connections and enable them to persist and thrive. Scholars who engage in research that focus on race, gender, and education could discover strategies to understand identity formations and socialization mechanisms that encourage Black women to persist. To ensure degree completion and success, universities can develop resources to provide Black women in graduate programs with the space to practice the necessary spiritual, physical, and social exercises. Identifying the priming stimuli and mechanisms underlying the intersection of race, gender, and social support is only useful if it provides insight into possible approaches to understanding and minimizing the effects of social marginalization. Specifically, Black women at the graduate level as they could offer insight regarding key experiences that permit them to persist through graduate education to combat their gross underrepresentation.

REFERENCES

Beasley, M. A., & Fischer, M. J. (2012). Why they leave: the impact of stereotype threat on the attrition of women and minorities from science, math and engineering majors. *Social Psychology of Education, 15*(2012), 427–448.

Beoku-Betts, J. (2004). African women pursuing graduate studies in the sciences: Racism, gender bias, and third world marginality. *NWSA Journal, 16*(1), 116–135. https://doi.org/10.2979/NWS.2004.16.1.116

Bertrand-Jones, T., Wilder, J., & Osborne-Lampkin, L. (2013). Employing a Black feminist approach to doctoral advising: Preparing Black women for the professoriate. *The Journal of Negro Education, 82*(3), 326–338.

Breakwell, G. M., & Beardsell, S. (1992). Gender, parental and peer influences upon science attitudes and activities. *Public Understanding of Science, 1*(2), 183–197. https://doi.org/10.1088/0963-6625/1/2/003

Brewer, R. (1999). Theorizing race, class and gender: The new scholarship of Black feminist intellectuals and Black women's labor. *Race, Gender & Class, 6*(2), 29–47.

Brickhouse, N. W., Lowery, P., & Schultz, K. (2000). What kind of a girl does science? The construction of school science identities. *Journal of Research in Science Teaching, 37*(5), 441–458.

C. Bullock, E. (2017). Only STEM can save us? Examining race, place, and STEM education as property. *Educational Studies, 53*(6), 628–641.

Carlone, H. B., & Johnson, A. (2007). Understanding the science experiences of successful women of color: Science identity as an analytic lens. *Journal of Research in Science Teaching, 44*(8), 1187–1218.

Charleston, L. J., Adserias, R. P., Lang, N., & Jackson, J. F. L. (2014). Intersectionality and STEM: The role of race and gender in the academic pursuits of African American women in STEM. *Journal of Progressive Policy & Practice, 2*(3), 17–37.

Chen, X. (2013). *STEM attrition: College students' paths into and out of stem fields (NCES2014-001)*. Washington, DC: National Center for Education Statistics, Institute of Education Sciences, U.S. Department of Education.

Collins, P. H. (2000). *Black feminist thought: Knowledge, consciousness, and the politics of empowerment* (2nd ed.). New York, NY: Routledge.

Colaizzi, P. F. (1978). Psychological research as the phenomenological views it. In R. Vaile & M. King (Eds.), *Existential phenomenological alternatives for psychology* (pp. 48–71). New York, NY: Oxford University Press.

Creswell, J. (2003). *Research design: Qualitative, quantitative, and mixed methods approaches* (2nd ed.). Thousand Oaks, CA: SAGE.

Creswell, J. W. (2009). *Research design: Qualitative, quantitative, and mixed method approaches* (3rd ed.). Thousand Oaks, CA: SAGE.

Davis, K. (2008). Intersectionality as buzzword: A sociology of science perspective on what makes a feminist theory successful. *Feminist Theory, 9*(1), 67–85.

Dortch, D., & Patel, C. (2017). Black undergraduate women and their sense of belonging in STEM at predominantly White institutions. *NASPA Journal About Women in Higher Education, 10*(2), 202–215.

Englander, M. (2012). The interview: Data collection in descriptive phenomenological human scientific research. *Journal of Phenomenological Psychology, 43,* 13–35.

Farinde, A., & Lewis, C. (2012). The underrepresentation of African American female students in STEM fields: Implications for classroom teachers. *US-China Education Review, 2*(4), 421–431.

Giogi, A. (2009). *The descriptive phenomenological method in psychology: A modified Husserlian approach*. Pittsburg, PA: Duquesne University Press.

Allum, J., & Okahana, H. (2015). *Graduate enrollment and degrees: 2004 to 2014*. Washington, DC: Council of Graduate Schools.

Haynes, C. M., & Joseph, N. M. (2016). Transforming the STEM system: Teaching that disrupts White institutional space. In N. M. Joseph, C. Haynes, & F. Cobb (Eds.), *Interrogating Whiteness and relinquishing power: White faculty's commitment to racial consciousness in STEM classrooms* (pp. 1–12). New York, NY: Peter Lang.

Huber, J., Whelan, K. K., & Clandinin, D. J. (2003) Children's narrative identity-making: becoming intentional about negotiating classroom spaces. *Journal of Curriculum Studies, 35*(3), 303–318. https://doi.org/10.1080/00220270210157623

Herrnstein, R. J., & Murray, C. (1994). *Bell Curve: Intelligence and class structure in American life*. New York, NY: Free Press.

Jett, C. C. (2019). Mathematical persistence among four African American male graduate students: A critical race analysis of their experiences. *Journal for Research in Mathematics Education, 50*(3), 311–340.

Johnson, A., Brown, J., Carlone, H., & Cuevas, A. K. (2011), Authoring identity amidst the treacherous terrain of science: A multiracial feminist examination of the journeys of three women of color in science. *Journal of Research in Science Teaching, 48*, 339–366.

Jones, S., & McEwen, M. (2000). A conceptual model of multiple dimensions of identity. *Journal of College Student Development, 41*(4), 405–414.

Joseph, J. (2012). From one culture to another: Years one and two of graduate school for African American women in the STEM fields. *International Journal of Doctoral Studies, 7,* 125–143.

Joseph, N. M., Hailu, M., & Boston, D. (2017). Black women's and girls' persistence in the P–20 mathematics pipeline: Two decades of children, youth, and adult education research. *Review of Research in Education, 41*(1), 203–227.

Kroger, J. (2015). Identity development through adulthood: The move toward "wholeness." https://doi.org/10.1093/oxfordhb/9780199936564.013.004

Kvale, S., & Brinkmann, S. (2009). *InterViews: Learning the craft of qualitative research interviewing* (2nd ed.). Thousand Oaks, CA: SAGE.

Lee, J. T. (2002). More than ability: Gender and personal relationships influence science and technology involvement. *Sociology of Education, 75*(4), 349–373.

Lieblich, A., Tuval-Mashiach, R., & Zilber, T. (1998). *Narrative research: Readings, analysis, interpretation.* Thousand Oaks, CA: SAGE.

Longfield, A., Romas, J., & Irwin, J. D. (2006). The self-worth, physical and social activities of graduate students: A qualitative study. *College Student Journal, 40*(2), 282–292.

Maxwell, J. A. (1996). *Qualitative research design: An interactive approach.* Thousand Oaks, CA: SAGE.

Merolla, D. M., Serpe, R. T., Stryker, S., & Schultz, P. W. (2012). Structural precursors to identity processes: The role of proximate social structures. *Social Psychology Quarterly, 75*(2), 149–172.

McGee, E. O., & Bentley, L. (2017). The troubled success of Black women in STEM. *Cognition and Instruction, 35*(4), 265–289.

Merolla, D. M., & Serpe, R. T. (2013). STEM enrichment programs and graduate school matriculation: the role of science identity salience. *Social Psychology of Education: An International Journal, 16*(4), 575–597. https://doi.org/10.1007/s11218-013-9233-7

Morton, T. R. (2020). A phenomenological and ecological perspective on the influence of undergraduate research experiences on Black women's persistence in STEM at an HBCU. *Journal of Diversity in Higher Education.* Advance online publication. https://doi.org/10.1037/dhe0000183

Morales, E. E. (2008). Exceptional Female students of color: Academic resilience and gender in higher education. *Innovative Higher Education, 33,* 197–213. https://doi.org/10.1007/s10755-008-9075-y

Morton, T. R., & Parsons, E. C. (2018). # BlackGirlMagic: The identity conceptualization of Black women in undergraduate STEM education. *Science Education, 102*(6), 1363–1393.

National Center for Science and Engineering Statistics (NCSES), National Science Foundation. (2017). *Survey of Doctorate Recipients, 2015 (SDR 2015).* Arlington, VA. Retrieved June 5, 2019, from https://ncsesdata.nsf.gov/doctoratework/

Ortiz, N. A., Morton, T. R., Miles, M. L., & Roby, R. S. (2020). What about us? Exploring the challenges and sources of support influencing Black students' STEM Identity development in postsecondary education. *The Journal of Negro Education*, *88*(3), 311–326.

Osmond, M. W., & Thorne, B. (1993). Feminist theories: The social construction of gender in families and society. In P. G. Boss, W. J. Doherty, R. Larossa, W. R. Schumm, & S. S. Steinmetz (Eds.), *Sourcebook of family theories and methods: A contextual approach* (pp. 591–622). New York, NY: Plenum Press.

Patton, M. Q. (2002). *Qualitative research & evaluation methods* (3rd ed.). Thousand Oaks, CA: SAGE.

Patton, M. (1990). *Qualitative evaluation and research methods* (2nd ed.). Newbury Park, CA: SAGE.

Pierce, C. (1995). Stress analogs of racism and sexism: Terrorism, torture, and disaster. In C. Willie, P. Rieker, B. Kramer, & B. Brown (Eds.), *Mental health, racism, and sexism* (pp. 277–293). Pittsburgh, PA: University of Pittsburgh Press.

Price, C. A. (1996). *Women and retirement: The unexplored transition* (Unpublished doctoral dissertation). University of Georgia, Athens, GA.

Ridgeway, M. L. (2019). A narrative of a developing Black critical STEM education researcher. *Taboo 18: 1-Full Issue*, 157.

Russell, M. L., & Atwater, M. M. (2005). Traveling the road to success: A discourse on persistence throughout the science pipeline with African American students at a predominantly white institution. *Journal of Research in Science Teaching*, *42*, 691–715. https://doi.org/10.1002/tea.20068

Sloan, A., & Bowe, B. (2014). Phenomenology and hermeneutic phenomenology: The philosophy, the methodologies, and using hermeneutic phenomenology to investigate lecturers' experiences of curriculum design. *Quality & Quantity*, *48*(3), 1291–1303.

Stratton, V. (n.d.) Engaging girls in STEM starts in kindergarten. *Education and Career News*. Retrieved March 15, 2020, from https://www.educationandcareernews.com/stem-education/engaging-girls-in-stem-starts-in-kindergarten/

Strauss, A. L. (1987). *Qualitative analysis for social scientists*. New York, NY: Cambridge University Press.

Strauss, A., & Corbin, J. (1990). *Basics of qualitative research: Grounded theory procedures and techniques*. Newbury Park, CA: SAGE.

Syed, M., & Chemers, M. M. (2011). Ethnic minorities and women in STEM: Casting a wide net to address a persistent social problem. *Journal of Social Issues*, *67*(3), 435–441. https://doi.org/10.1111/j.1540-4560.2011.01708.x

Thompson, J. (2014). Engaging girls' sociohistorical identities in science. *Journal of the Learning Sciences*, *23*(3), 392–446. https://doi.org/10.1080/10508406.2014.888351

Tyler, A. L., & Muhammad, L. (2014) Race, gender, and single parenting: Dismantling the "invisible" myth around intellectual Black female scholars. In S. D. Hancock, A. Allen, & C. W. Lewis (Eds.), *Race, research, and the politics of schooling: Culturalized perspectives on autoethnography*. Charlotte, NC: Information Age.

Wong, B. (2012). Identifying with science: A case study of two 13-year-old British Asian 'high achieving working class' schoolgirls. *International Journal of Science Education, 34*, 43–65.

Wright, B. L., Ford, D. Y., & Young, J. L. (2017). Ignorance or indifference? Seeking excellence and equity for under-represented students of color in gifted education. *Global Education Review, 4*(1), 45–60.

CHAPTER 7

STRENGTHENING STEM IDENTITIES

Combatting Curriculum Trauma in African American Students

Stephen D. Hancock and Michelle B. Pass
University of North Carolina, Charlotte

INTRODUCTION

If you conduct a google search on "what is the heart of the school" the results overwhelmingly favors the library and librarians. In fact, in many schools the library is in the center or a prominent location of the school building. While the library (virtual or physical) is an important and necessary part of every school, the curriculum is a more authentic representation of the heart of the school. Because the ultimate purpose of schooling is to develop an educated population through curriculum content, the curriculum is the most important nonhuman element in schools. It is not only important as a source of knowledge, but it also has the power to shape intellectual and academic identities as well to validate knowledge, nurture images, promote cultures, and reshape worldviews. Linkson (1999) defines worldview as "the way in which various sets of assumptions under-

Seeing The HiddEn Minority, pp. 121–131
Copyright © 2020 by Information Age Publishing
All rights of reproduction in any form reserved.

lying human existence form a set of beliefs which explain the meaning of life" (p. 43). Therefore, the underlying purpose of the curriculum is to promote a set of beliefs and knowledge deemed as valid and superior to the omitted beliefs and knowledge. In short, the curriculum has the power to determine the current and future pathways of the students that consume it. Thus, it is critically important to deeply analyze the cultural worldview of the curriculum in order to ensure strong academic and intellectual identities for all students who participate in it. In the United States the cultural worldview that develops curricula is White and often male. In fact, Cohen, Spillane, and Peurach (2018) suggests that early public schools (and curricula) were managed by white men from rural backgrounds. While schools are a much more culturally diverse place, the worldview of curricula remains grounded in a White male worldview. Unfortunately, curriculum images, knowledge, and values grounded in a White male worldview often marginalize and disenfranchise the identity of non-White students. In this chapter we explore how the curriculum, and specifically STEM curriculum, marginalizes African American students through the omission of positive images, inventions, and innovations of African American STEM professionals. The underlying supposition of this chapter is that bias causes trauma.

IDENTITY DEFERRED

George Johnson was born in 1921 in Cincinnati Ohio. As the world healed from World War I, young George grew up in a loving family with 10 siblings. His parents nurtured all of their children to do their best and George was no exception. His father was a well-known music teacher in the Black community and in the early years he enjoyed making music with his family. George was described as brilliant, nice, and a lover of science. However, he lost 100% of his hearing at 12 years old. In 1933 a hearing disability created challenging and traumatic realities that required him to overcome school, curriculum, and social hurdles. Despite deafness his mother demanded he stay in regular classes and attend school with his siblings. As a result, George became a master lip reader and did not lose any intellectual ground. Even with the sudden trauma of deafness, George's interest in science never waned. With a strong family network, intellectual prowess, a relevant curriculum, and good teachers George graduated high school at the top of his class. After high school, he entered The Ohio State University, graduated at the top of his class, and became a nuclear scientist. In the early 1950s he was the first and only African American nuclear physicist to work at the United States military research center at the Los Alamos National Laboratory. In 1955 he was featured in Ebony magazine as a prominent scientist.

Forty-six years after George Johnson graduated from high school in 1939 his oldest granddaughter graduated from a high school in Charlottesville, VA. Gina Carter was a self-proclaimed math geek and like her grandfather's science intelli-

gence she had a high mathematic aptitude. Gina's schooling, however, was different from her grandfather's. George Johnson attended a high school for Black students in the 1930s that undoubtedly nurtured his science intelligence with a curriculum that minimized the White male worldview. Unfortunately, Gina attended a predominantly White high school that promoted the White male worldview curriculum without mentioning the diverse ideals of mathematicians all over the world. In fact, as an honors and advanced math student, Gina didn't know the contributions of Katherine Johnson, Euphemia Haynes, or Majorie Lee Browne and thus was not able to strengthen her identity as a mathematician. Through teachers and the curriculum, Gina was not nurtured in STEM identities and thus disenfranchised from her dream of becoming a statistician or accountant. And while she hailed from a scientific pioneer, her grandfather's work was never mentioned in the curriculum nor was she given opportunities to share his accomplishments. Fortunately, the inspiration of her grandfather, support of her family, and self-determination, has compelled Gina into a fulfilling career as a financial auditor.

It is apparent in this story that George Johnson benefited from a curriculum that supported his identity, behavior, and budding knowledge as a scientist. We can postulate that in the late 1930s George did not learn with the latest equipment, textbooks, or most educated teachers. However, the curriculum affirmed his intelligence, identity, and love for science. Unfortunately, Gina was not afforded a curriculum that promoted Black women as mathematicians, nor was she introduced to multiple pathways to math studies and careers. Her identity as a mathematician was deferred until through determination, she became an auditor. This is to say that while many African American children matriculate through 13 years of a curriculum that marginalize, criminalize, and omit the work and contributions of African Americans, some may still rise to meet their dreams. However, the trauma still lingers. Despite Gina's current success she is still saddened by how she was treated in high school. The dream deferred continues to haunt her. The "what if" is a trauma statement that she will live with her entire life. What if her high school curriculum promoted the accomplishments of Black female mathematicians beside White males? What if the work of her grandfather was part of the science curriculum? What if her counselor saw the math genius in her? How far might Gina have gone? How stronger would our communities be if all students were included in the curriculum? Unfortunately, the curriculum is designed and written to support a White male worldview and subsequently induces identity trauma for those that don't see themselves in through White male lens.

TRAUMA DEFINED

The Substance Abuse and Mental Health Services Administration (as cited in West, Day, Somers, & Baroni, 2014) defines trauma as caused by "an event, series of events, or set of circumstances that is experienced by an individual as physically or emotionally harmful or threatening and that has lasting adverse effects on the individual's functioning and physical social, emotional, or spiritual well-being" (West, Day, Somers, & Baroni, 2014). We submit that trauma can also happen in micro and macro incidents and in any location or experience. We contend that micro and macro traumas happen when unfavorable events, conversations, interactions, and persistently negative depictions of self are endemic in an environment.

The Oxford American Dictionary defines trauma as a deeply distressing or disturbing experience. The Massachusetts Advocates for Children organization suggest that persistent stresses can hinder the healthy development of peer and adult relationships as well as negatively impact a youth's ability to communicate and organize information (West et al., 2014). Further, Cook et al. (2005) suggest that the effects of children who are subject to long term maltreatment can cause emotional imbalance.

Trauma is a deeply personal phenomenon that can conversely be trivialized, misrepresented, and ignored when it's not understood. Trauma is manifested from many different stimuli. Unfortunately, stimuli that are supposed to be positive may produce deeper traumatic response. For example, a circus or birthday clown can be a traumatic experience for individuals who find it an intensely frightening figure. Trauma can also be stimulated by seemingly innocuous events, material, activities, and experiences. Thus, it is important that educators critically exam schooling to identity practices and material that might contribute to traumatizing students.

CURRICULUM AS CENTER OF SCHOOLING

The curriculum is the center of the education endeavor. Without the curriculum there would be no reason for children and adults to gather in a space for 6–8 hours a day for 185 days. In addition, the curriculum is simultaneously the most important and least critically applied part of schooling. For example, while there is plethora of data, research articles, and even curriculum guides and models to support the application of a more antibiased and thus antitraumatic curriculum, local and state education entities continue to rely on for-profit companies to develop culturally detrimental curriculum.

Curriculum marginalization of nondominant populations is evident in every subject, but is especially true in STEM curricula or subjects based in math, science, technology, and engineering. Cannady, Greenwald, and Harris (2014) suggest that the entire metaphor about STEM education-to-career is oversimplified, too narrow, and alienates alternative pathways to STEM studies and professions. Linkson (1999) contends the cultural bias is endemic in science curriculum in Western nations because it is inextricably tied to progress. Aikenhead and Jegede (1998, as cited in Linkson, 1999), suggest when the culture of science curriculum is in opposition to a student's worldview, it will undoubtedly marginalize and demean the student's belief and knowledge system (Linkson, 1999).

Worldview is important in curriculum because it undergirds belief systems and life meaning. Similar to the fight between creationist and evolutionist, cultures come to schools with different assumptions and worldviews concerning the use and application of math, science, engineering, and technology. The best way to teach nondominant students is to contextualize their STEM learning in relevant life experiences that support their worldview. We argue that curriculum is the center of schooling and should be inclusive of multiple perspectives and contributions.

The contributions and worldview of African Americans to the fields of science, technology, engineering and math, remain largely omitted from American history and science curriculum. All students, and specifically African American students, would benefit from a comprehensive curriculum that support the contributions that African Americans have made in STEM. In fact, incorporating African American STEM achievements would be emotionally and intellectually transformative for all students and would deconstruct the stereotypical and accepted views of scientists as White, middle class, men. For example, the positive and lasting impact of an African American centered STEM curriculum on African American students can be found in the Greene Scholars program in the Bay Area. This STEM focused program produces 100% high school graduates that pursue four-year college, community college, or military experiences. These scholars participate in dynamic and innovative science fairs that rival state, national, and international science competitions. African American students in the program are not only competent in STEM concepts they are confident in their STEM identities.

In an effort to support both competence and confidence in STEM, it is important that African American students are exposed to innovative and seminal STEM achievements and people. For example, Rebecca Lee Crumpler who in 1864 became the first African American woman to earn a medical degree in the United States and was known for her work with former enslaved Africans in the postwar south. Her book, *A Book of Medical Discourses,* written in 1883, was one of the first publications about medicine written by an African American. The contributions of African Americans are not limited to medicine. In 1876 Edward Alexander Bouchet became the first African American to earn a PhD in physics. Dr. Bouchet was the son of former enslaved Africans who went on to become the first Black student to be nominated to Phi Beta Kappa Honor Society and the first Black student to graduate from Yale. Dr. Bouchet went on to teach Black students during a time when leaders including Booker T. Washington were advocating for Black students to pursue vocational and technical training. Dr. Bouchet was a clear example that Black students should not be limited to manual trades but were capable of academic and scientific professions.

African Americans are momentous contributors to scientific and medical advances. For example, Percy Lavon Julian was born in 1899 and despite only completing the eighth grade, Percy went on to earn his high school diploma while attending college. He graduated first in his class and went on to earn a master's degree and PhD in chemistry. As the grandson of former enslaved Africans, Dr. Julian is a pioneer in the chemical and pharmaceutical discoveries. His seminal work was first in synthesizing medical drugs including cortisone and hydrocortisone. Dr. Julian's chemical advances in the field of pharmacology have provided drugs to treat arthritis and other inflammatory diseases. In addition, he also developed physostigmine which is a foundational chemical used to treat glaucoma. In 1953 he went on to establish his own chemical companies in the U.S. and Mexico. He later sold Julian Laboratories to pharmaceutical giants, Smith Kline and UpJohn for 2.3 million, making him one of the first Black millionaires. Dr. Julian received more than 130 chemical patents throughout his career, was elected to the National Inventors Hall of Fame in 1990, and in 1999 his discoveries were recognized in the top 25 achievements in the history of American chemistry. Dr. Julian's contributions extended beyond the laboratory as he was a staunch advocate for the rights of African Americans. Dr. Julian's passion for the education of African Americans led him to teach at two historically Black universities, Fisk University and Howard University. Dr. Julian's life was the focus of a 2007 documentary film made for PBS's Nova series, entitled *Forgotten Genius*.

The curriculum acts as gatekeeper to the knowledge and experiences that students receive in schools. A mono-perspective curriculum produces intellectual trauma that last a lifetime for all students. Thus it is salient to include and study the worldviews, contributions, pictures, innovations, and names of African American STEM professional in an effort to support STEM identities for all students. Unfortunately, the omission of African American STEM professionals and the overrepresentation of White men in STEM, contribute to the concept of curriculum trauma.

CURRICULUM TRAUMA: A FRAMEWORK

The underrepresentation or omission of African American STEM professionals in the curriculum is directly linked to the underrepresentation of African America students pursuing STEM majors. In fact, the dearth of African American students graduating with STEM degrees and entering the STEM workforce has been the topic of numerous research studies, receiving significant attention inside and outside academia (Chen & Soldner, 2013; Hurtado, Newman, Tran, & Chang, 2010; Mau, 2016). Researchers posit that African American students lack engagement in STEM due to their inability to see themselves as "scientists."

Archer et al. (2015) in their research study explored the science aspirations and engagements of African American students ages 10–14 years old. They found that African American students were more likely than students from other ethnic backgrounds to think that someone would have to be "brainy" to be a scientist. The students believed they could not "do science" because science was "very hard." African American students tend to be more broadly affected by the stereotypical images of scientists they have been exposed to in school and in popular media and therefore are unable to form a science identity because they believe they lack the intelligence or aptitude to "do science" (Scantlebury, 2007). The stereotypical images of STEM professionals as White men are overrepresented in curriculum, social discourse, and media. We contend that curriculum trauma goes beyond STEM, is manifested from many different pedagogical stimuli, and is a deeply personal phenomenon that can conversely be trivialized, misrepresented, and ignored when it's not understood. Unfortunately, for many African American students the curriculum represents a stimulus that can produce both intellectual and emotional trauma. Curriculum trauma can be characterized as the discourses of overrepresentation and omission.

The curriculum trauma framework is developed using Miller's (2017) research on the overrepresentation of Whites in school and social material and the omission (or diminished representation) of nondominant peoples in school and social material. I, Hancock, have extended this work to include the reality of positive and negative overrepresentation and omission as it relates to maintaining White supremacy and African American inferiority in curriculum offerings. The curriculum trauma framework encompasses the concepts of overrepresentation and omission as fundamental but intentional decisions of curriculum developers. These intentional decisions are unfortunately made based on a lack of cultural competence and historical intelligence.

The framework dissects the discourse of overrepresentation into two subcategories that include positive overrepresentation for Whites (pofW1) and negative overrepresentation for African Americans (nofAA1). These categories are further deconstructed to reveal the outcomes of the subcategories pofW1 and nofAA1. The subcategory pofW1 the outcomes have beneficial impact on academic identity resulting in internalized superiority and academic longevity. Conversely, the subcategory nofAA1 is disconfirming for African American academic identity development as it promotes internalized inferiority and academic fatigue.

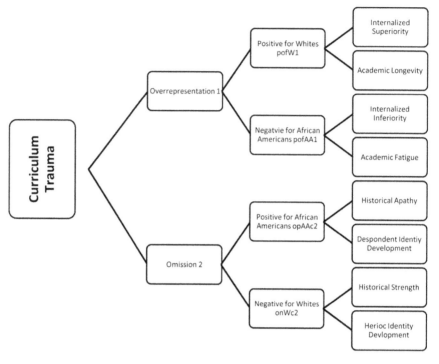

Figure 7.1. Curriculum Trauma Framework.

Similarly, the discourse of omission is dissected into two subcategories described as omission of positive African American contributions (opAAc2) and omission of negative contributions of Whites (onWc2). The outcomes of the subcategory opAAc2 include the development of apathy for learning history and a negative self-image. The outcomes of subcategory onWc2 produce a sense of strength in historical knowledge and a heroic identity complex. Unfortunately, the fragile reality of these outcomes can set up White students for curriculum trauma if they are exposed to comprehensive curriculum offerings.

In this chapter it is not possible to comprehensively discuss the various components of curriculum trauma. Table 7.1 is entitled Overrepresentation/Omission Discourses and it provides curriculum descriptions of the discourses as well as possible outcomes of the subcategories of each discourse on both African American and White students.

Curriculum trauma can occur in micro and macro incidents and in any subject or learning experience within the classroom. For example, being the only African American student in class during discussions on civil rights is often traumatic. African American students are often expected to speak for the entire complex and multicultural African American community. In addition, curriculum trauma experiences happen in conversations, pedagogical interactions, and persistently negative depictions and omitted contributions of African Americans in the curriculum.

Table 7.1.
Overrepresentation/Omission Discourses

Discourse of Overrepresentation 1		
	Curriculum Product	**Outcome**
Positive *Overrepresentation* *of the contributions* *and impact of Whites* *(pofW1)*	Overrepresentation of Whites in dominant positions in literature and pictures	Internalized White Privilege
	Overrepresentation of Whites as good, smart, and right (White worldview)	Internalized Racial Superiority
	Overrepresentation of Whites as center of history, math, science	Reify White Dominance
Negative *Overrepresentation* *of the actions and* *statistics of African* *Americans (nofAA1)*	Overrepresentation of African Americans as socially inferior	Internalized Racial Inferiority
	Overrepresentation of African Americans as academic failures (tests, AIG, etc.)	Reify African American Intellectually Inferiority
	Overrepresentation of African Americans in discipline referrals	Pygmalion Effect on Expectations
Discourse of Omission 2		
Comprehensive *Omission of* *Positive actions and* *contributions of* *African Americans* *(opAAc2)*	Omission of endemic and continuous African American success in the curriculum.	Academic Fatigue
	Omission of African American contribution to Math, Science, Literature, Art, History, Medicine, Business, and Education.	Academic Fatigue
	Omission of the Afrocentric perspective or worldview in curriculum.	Internalized Racial Inferiority
Comprehensive *Omission of Negative* *actions and impact of* *Whites (onWc2)*	Omission of Whites as criminals, bad, or wrong (murderers, genocide, enslavers)	Historical Apathy
	Omission of Whites and the history of ill-gotten wealth	Delusion of White Work Ethic & Meritocracy
	Omission of Whites and the support of Institutional Racism	Delusion of Governmental Fairness for all

COMBATTING CURRICULUM TRAUMA: CONCLUSION

Parsons (2008) proposes using culturally respectful and "caring" approaches to engage African American students in science. Pedagogical practices that validate and incorporate the cultural capital of urban youth can make science engaging and relatable for African American students (Basu & Barton, 2007). These approaches assist African American students in forming science identities. The curriculum must be dismantled and redesigned to include flexibility where African American students can use their home knowledge, worldviews, and cultural resources to engage in STEM concepts, principles, and theories. Pedagogical practices that engage the epistemological realities, historical contributions, and STEM advances of African American students can be transformative as they validate STEM identities. I contend that when the experience and epistemologies African American students are aligned with the curriculum only then will an affirming academic relationship will be formed (Hancock, 2017). Once again, it is important to include and study the worldviews, contributions, pictures, innovations, and names of African American STEM professional in an effort to support STEM identities for all students.

In order to combat curriculum trauma and engage African American students in STEM, it is important to promote a curriculum that support African Americans as STEM professionals and innovators. In addition, schools must adopt curricular that are undergirded in multiple perspectives and comprehensive representations of artist, business pioneers, educators, medical professionals, innovators, literary geniuses, philosophers, scientist, engineers, mathematicians, and technology inventors.

REFERENCE

Archer, L., Dewitt, J. & Osbourne, J. (2015). Is science for us? Black students' and parents' views of science and science careers. *Science Education, 99*(2), 199–237.

Basu, S. J., & Barton, A. C. (2007). Developing a sustained interest in science among urban minority youth. *Journal of Research in Science Teaching, 44*(3), 466–489.

Cannady, M. A., Greenwald, E., & Harris, K. N. (2014). Problematizing the STEM pipeline metaphor: Is the STEM pipeline metaphor serving our students and the STEM workforce? *Science Education, 98*(3), 443–460.

Cohen, D. K., Spillane, J. P., & Peurach, D. J. (2018). The dilemmas of educational reform. *Educational Researcher, 47*(3), 204–212.

Cook, A., Spinazzola, J., Ford, J., Lanktree, C., Blaustein, M., Cloitre, M., ... van Der Kolk, B. (2005). Complex trauma in children and adolescents. *Psychiatric Annals, 35*(5), 390–398.

Chen, X., & Soldner, M. (2013). STEM attrition: college students' paths into and out of STEM fields. Statistical Analysis Report. *Report NCES 2014–001, US Dept. of Education*.

Hancock, S. D. (2017). Double image, single identity: Constructive academic relationship in multiethnic classrooms. In S. D. Hancock & C. A. Warren (Eds.), *White women's work: Examining the intersectionality of teaching, identity, and race* (pp. 71–86). Charlotte, NC: Information Age Publishing.

Hurtado, S., Newman, C. B., Tran, M. C., & Chang, M. J. (2010). Improving the rate of success for underrepresented racial minorities in STEM fields: Insights from a national project. *New Directions for Institutional Research, 148*, 5–15.

Linkson, M. (1999). Some issues in providing culturally appropriate science curriculum support for indigenous students. *Australian Science Teachers' Journal, 45*(1), 41–48.

Mau, W. C. J. (2016). Characteristics of US students that pursued a STEM major and factors that predicted their persistence in degree completion. *Universal Journal of Educational Research, 4*(6), 1495–1500.

Miller, E. (2017). The murky and mediated experience of white identities in early childhood. In S. D. Hancock & C. A. Warren (Eds.), *White women's work: Examining the intersectionality of teaching, identity, and race* (pp. 123–144). Charlotte, NC: Information Age Publishing.

Parsons, E. C. (2008). Learning contexts, black cultural ethos, and the science-achievement of African American students in an urban middle school. *Journal of Research in Science Teaching, 45*(6), 665–683.

Scantlebury, K. (2007). Outsiders within. Urban African-American girls' identity and science In W.-M. Roth & M. Tobin (Eds.), *Science, learning and identity*. Rotterdam, Netherlands: Sense.

West, S., Day, A., Somers, C., & Baroni, B. (2014). Student perspectives on how trauma experiences manifest in the classroom: Engaging court-involved youth in the development of a trauma-informed teaching curriculum. *Children and Youth Services Review, 38*(C), 58–65.

CHAPTER 8

UNEARTHING FACTORS THAT CONTRIBUTE TO DISTORTED SCIENCE IDENTITIES IN AFRICAN AMERICAN WOMEN

Ansley Booker
Mercer University

This chapter seeks to unearth how gender, racial, social, and academic identity factors affect persistence in STEM disciplines for African American women. Brickhouse, Lowery, and Schultz (2000) have stated that African American girls must determine an identity in a STEM field as early as middle school to ensure a definitive career path. Carlone and Johnson (2007) noted that the early development of a *science identity* provided a solid foundation for future career success. However, researchers have suggested that the dearth of Black women in STEM is not due to their intellectual capacity but instead due to the pitfalls of the American education system to under-educate, disengage and underutilize them through the course of the STEM academic pipeline (Farinde & Lewis, 2012; Johnson, Brown, Carlone, & Cuevas, 2011; Ko, Kachchaf, Ong, & Hodari, 2013; Margolis, Goode, & Bernier, 2011; Syed & Chemers, 2011). The "leaky" STEM pipeline is a metaphor used to describe the transition from education to

Seeing The HiddEn Minority, pp. 133–143
Copyright © 2020 by Information Age Publishing
All rights of reproduction in any form reserved.

career. During this transition, many underrepresented minorities specifically African American women are lost during this transition. The term to "leak out" describes those that fall out or leak from the pipeline between the bachelors and masters level or that may not transition to a STEM career (Garbee, 2017). Those that survive the "leaky" pipeline and matriculate through college have attributed their lack of persistence to social isolation, academic difficulties, and financial stresses that were based on their racial identity (Buzzetto-Moore, Ukoha, & Rustagi, 2010; George Neale, Van Horne, & Malcolm, 2001; Jackson & Charleston, 2012). Those that finish the continuum unto career opportunities find themselves at a crossroads trying to navigate multiple social identities as "double bind" including that of a woman, an African American, and as a scientist. The double-bind is described as the difficulties experienced by women specifically minority women due to sexism and racism in their STEM careers which are often dominated by white and Asian males (Ong, Wright, Espinosa, & Orfield, 2011). Several researchers suggest that women are faced with a difficult task of balancing their career and family responsibilities while simultaneously navigating traditional gender roles and racial stereotypes (Cech, Rubineau, Silbey, & Seron, 2011; Charleston, Adserias, Lang, & Jackson, 2014; Ko et al., 2013).

Compounded by external pressures of belonging to more than one social group, women find difficulty in penetrating the "glass ceiling" while facing difficulty attaining promotions and tenure in academic settings as compared to their male counterparts. Other factors that have affected science identity at various stages include the reinforcement of stereotypical gender roles, implicit bias, and culture norms that have led to a "chilly" STEM environment. The "chilly" environment is cultivated by racism and sexism imparted by male students, professors, and co-workers who have led to increasing difficulty in African American women establishing gender, racial and social identities in STEM careers (Settles, 2014). This "chilly" STEM environment is often emphasized by female undergraduate students. These women reported experiences of a negative climate that was heightened by a competitive, alienating and hostile environment. This resulted in greater depression and lower self-esteem and poorer academic performance perceptions for these undergraduates (Settles, 2014). The "chilly" environment is attributed to the isolation experienced by these women as a result of stereotypes, racism, and sexism. Lastly, researchers found that the intersections of Black women's racial, gender, and scientific identities may hinder a Black women's ability to develop a scientist identity because of the conflicting messages Black women and girls receive from various educational sources (Charleston, Adserias, Lang, & Jackson, 2014). In addition, other research has found that many minority women in STEM have a strong connection to younger STEM generations and therefore use their influence to improve conditions from them through recruitment, volunteerism, and charity work (Charleston et al., 2014; Ko et al., 2013).

How does one subscribe to an identity? Burke and Stets (2009) describes identity as a set of meanings that define or characterize a person in terms of their role (role identities), group of category memberships (social identities) or unique individual characteristics (person identities). The question of how does a young African American girl identify as a scientist? Research has shown that African American girls must determine identity in the STEM as early as the fourth grade to ensure a definitive career path. According to Steinke (2017), research notes that girls tend to lose interest in STEM by the age of 12. In addition, girls also report being less interested in STEM careers than boys at an earlier age (Farkas & Leaper, 2016; Riegle-Crumb, Moore, & Ramos-Wada, 2011; Robnett & Leaper, 2013). However, due to several external factors including academic underpreparedness, gender stereotypes and lack of visual role models many young girls fail to establish strong STEM identities.

External factors also contributing to a young girls' science identity include media representation. Many images portrayed in the media have not actively highlighted women as a scientist or in STEM careers, especially women of color. Perceptions of women are filtered through stereotypes. An example of such stereotype is that women are perceived as less intelligent and less competent in math and science as compared to their male counterparts (Lane, Goh, & Driver-Linn, 2012; Shih, Pittinsky, & Ambady, 1999). Moreover, cultural stereotypes have associated the following characteristics with scientists stating that they are objective, rational, and single-minded, which are consistent with prescribed norms for men, but are not easily associated with gender stereotypes and prescribed norms for women (Barbercheck, 2001; Diekman & Steinberg, 2013; Fiske, Cuddy, Glick, & Xu, 2002). Therefore, in order to ensure accurate representation of women in STEM society must embrace changes socially.

Social identity is one of the most critical variables in assuring minority women's STEM academic and career goals (Ong et al., 2011). Carlone and Johnson (2007) noted that the development of a science identity provided a solid foundation for future career success among minority women. This was established based on three science identity trajectories including research scientist, altruistic scientist, and disrupted scientist. One of the significant findings of this study detailed the importance of having women scientists recognized by another science faculty as a scientist. In a study by Perez, Cromley, and Kaplan (2014) researchers explored the role of college students' identity development and motivational beliefs in predicting their chemistry achievement and intentions to leave science, technology, engineering, and math (STEM) majors. Findings suggest that if students made commitments to STEM careers after identity exploration, they were more likely to stay committed and motivated. This initial investigation of identity in conjunction with self-efficacy could slow the rates of attrition. Lastly, as determined by Parker (2013), many African American women were influenced by family factors and science identities. These women were affected by five themes including independence, support, the pressure to succeed, adaptations, and race and gender.

One important variable to consider when determining a science identity includes a review of the scientist's self-efficacy. "Self-efficacy refers to an individual's belief in his or her capacity to execute behaviors necessary to produce specific performance attainments" (Bandura, 1977, 1986, 1997). Also, early barriers to STEM attainment may result in lower levels of self-efficacy in science, math, and technology, and unfortunately low self-efficacy contributes to depressed levels of STEM degree attainment (Espinosa, 2008). When choosing a STEM major researchers found that prior achievement in mathematics contributed both significantly and positively to perceived math self-efficacy for underrepresented minorities, which in turn played a significant role in students' decisions to choose to STEM major (Wang, 2013). Considerable attention should be paid to early science and math achievement as it may be an early precursor to later developments in math and science self-efficacy (Riegle-Crumb, King, Grodsky, & Muller, 2012; Riegle-Crumb, Moore, & Ramos-Wada, 2011).

Figure 8.1 authored by Byers-Winston et al. (2016) suggests that there are several variables at play when deciding to pursue STEM degree attainment. She noted that person inputs and background/contextual affordances affect learning experiences (sources of efficacy). Those sources of efficacy including performance accomplishments, vicarious learning, social persuasion, and effective/emotional arousal then influence a student's research self-efficacy, science identity, and outcome expectations. As those variables interact with each other, they ultimately affect the students' interests, goals, and actions.

THEORETICAL FRAMEWORK

The *science identity model* can be utilized to determine a way in which a person decides to persist through a scientific discipline. Several studies have pointed to having a strong science identity as a key to understanding persistence, especially in minority groups' particularly African American women. Carlone and Johnson (2007) identified a *science identity model* based on 15 African American women in scientific careers. This model identified three variables that affected a scientist's development including competence, recognition, and performance, which were also influenced by their gender, race, and ethnicity. The study also noted that recognition

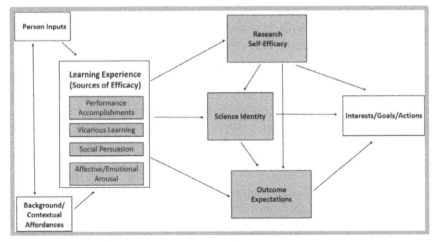

Source: Coauthors Drs. Anglea Byars-Winston and Jenna Rogers.

Figure 81. Modified social cognitive career theory model.

by others in the scientific community helps to promote matriculation for African American women in the STEM community (Steinke, 2017). Parker (2013) noted that science identity along with independence, support, the pressure to succeed, adaptations, and race and gender heavily influence African American women's persistence in STEM majors. Herrera, Hurtado, Garcia, and Gasiewski (2012) conducted a study in which 132 graduate students in the STEM and non-STEM communities were interviewed. From these interviews coupled with the science identity model, the researchers developed the *STEM identity model* (Steinke, 2017). The model also utilizes Jones and McEwens (2000) model of multiple social identities to explain the interactions between STEM identity and social identity. Herrera et al. (2012) noted that gender, race/ethnicity, religion/spiritually, mental/physical ability, socioeconomic status, sexual orientation, culture, and nationality/immigration status all were considered in social identities.

IMPLICIT BIAS

Black women are more likely than white women to express interest in majoring in science, technology, engineering, or mathematics (STEM) fields when they enter college, but they are less likely to earn degrees in these areas (O'Brien, Blodorn, Adams, Garcia, & Hammer, 2014). This expressed interest by minority women to achieve STEM degrees is important however

138   A. BOOKER

many barriers and obstacles present themselves including self-efficacy, lack of support, academic preparedness and gender bias which prevent them from obtaining such degrees. According to Williams, Phillips, and Hall (2015), gender bias is pushing women out of science, and that preference varies based on the women's race or ethnicity. The first pattern that demonstrates this is entitled Prove-it-Again. "Two-thirds of women interviewed, and two-thirds of the women surveyed, reported having to prove themselves over and over again- their success discounted, their expertise questioned." "Black women were considerably more likely than other women to report having to deal with this type of bias; three- fourths of black women did" (Williams et al., 2015, p. 5). The second pattern can be described as The Tightrope. Women found themselves walking a tightrope between being too feminine to be competent and too masculine to be likable. Fifty-three percent of women surveyed, who reportedly behaved as "masculine" received backlash for displaying stereotypical behavior. More than 34.1% of scientists surveyed reported feeling pressure to play a traditionally feminine role (Williams et al., 2015, p. 5). According to the study, only Black and Latina women were more susceptible to being viewed as angry when they failed to follow stereotypical norms. The third pattern is the Maternal Wall. The maternal wall is expressed when women lose advancement opportunities, have their competence questioned and are expected to work longer hours to compete with colleagues who do not have children (Williams et al., 2015). About two-thirds of all women scientists interviewed reported this type of bias.

Tug-of-War is the fourth pattern. Research has shown that women who encounter discrimination early in their careers distance themselves from other women (Williams et al., 2015). Williams also noted that this form of gender bias could cause dissemination among different generations of women. Three-fourths of women surveyed reported that women support each other in the work environment. About a fifth reported competing with colleagues for the "women's spot" (Williams et al., 2015, p. 6). Lastly, the fifth pattern is Isolation. This bias was discovered to affect Black and Latina women mainly. On the survey 42% of Black women agreed that "I feel that socially engaging with my colleagues may negatively affect my perceptions of competence" (Williams et al., 2015, p. 46) Almost half of the Black women (48%) and (47%) of Latinas report having been mistaken for administrative or custodial staff.

GLASS CEILING

"Female faculty (natural scientists) members reported more perceived gender discrimination in relation to hiring, promotion, salary, space, equipment, access to administrative staff, and graduate student or resident/fellow assignments as well as more sexual harassment compared to non-STEM faculty members" (Settles, Cortina, Buchanan, & Miner, 2013). The notion of the "glass obstacle course" captures the unequal gendered processes at work in women's graduate career including exclusion from the "Old Boys' Club," outright sexism, a lack of women role models, and difficult work-life choices. These obstacles are "glass" because they are often implicit and unanticipated, they are neither visible nor breakable (Federal Glass Ceiling Commission, 1995). Ideological and structural constraints, informal and formal biases, and active resistance or accommodations to them have shaped career pathways for women scientists and engineers. Such accumulated disadvantages can affect women's attrition from and satisfaction with their chosen STEM fields (De Welde & Laursen, 2011).

RECOMMENDATIONS

In order to eradicate the distorted science identities of African American women, several precautions must be taken to preserve the integrity of their fragile STEM identity. Literature has suggested that girls must be integrated into the STEM pipeline as early as third grade. Therefore, one recommendation is early intervention programs to introduce these young girls to STEM during the K–12 pipeline. The United States Department of Education and the Committee on STEM Education (CoSTEM) have committed to engage historically underrepresented groups in STEM and provide quality education and teacher preparedness with such incentives in the Race to the Top-District program. School districts must be compelled to invest in these grants along with faculty professional development to ensure a quality education for these individuals. In addition, the USDOE has also introduced the Ready-to-Learn Television grant competition to ensure the development of digital and social media with a STEM focus (Science, Technology, Engineering, and Math: Education for Global Leadership, 2015). This visual representation of STEM is a necessity in a society when STEM careers are not highly visualized. (Sheehy, 2012). In addition, the visual representation is also critical in helping Black girls and women establish a science identity, therefore, such programming and advertising should employ underrepresented minorities to ensure the persistence of such students.

In addition, institutions of higher education and employers must work tirelessly to ensure that women are not subjected to "chilly" STEM environment nor held captive by the "glass ceiling." Miner, Settles, Brady, and Pratt-Hyatt (2012) suggest that through strong organizational leadership, women may obtain a sense of belonging and inclusion, which may help

140 A. BOOKER

to lessen the impact of the negative outcomes previously mentioned. In order to ensure, the racism, sexism, and isolation felt in academia and the workplace administrators and employers must institute diversity and inclusivity training to help identity and eradiate bias. Training and education on Title IX policies based on gender discrimination and workplace performance must be implemented and maintained. Clear reporting procedures and consequences must be identified and demonstrated throughout the company and university. Buchanan, Settles, Hall, and O'Connor (2014) suggest the necessity for the firm and consistent organizational leaders that have a zero-tolerance towards this mistreat. Furthermore, a strong mentorship and leadership opportunities for women in academia and the career sector are important. Organizational leadership must employ, promote, hire, and award tenure to women as equally as men in addition to helping to close the gender pay gap in the STEM. Such practices will help shatter the "glass ceiling" and provide for a lucrative career field. Lastly, strong organization leadership paired with a shift in societal stereotypes and less science identity interference will help further improve recruitment and retention of women in STEM (Settles, 2014). In sum, there are multiple variables that affect a Black women's science identity, however, if societal stereotypes are contradicted, improvements in education for minorities are made, and organizations confront racism, sexism, and discrimination an increase in the number of women in STEM will surely follow.

REFERENCES

Bandura, A. (1977). Self-efficacy: Toward a unifying theory of behavioral change. *Psychological Review, 84*(2), 191–215.

Bandura, A. (1986). *Social foundations of thought and action: A social cognitive theory.* Englewood Cliffs, NJ: Prentice Hall.

Bandura, A. (1997). *Self-efficacy: The exercise of control.* New York, NY: W.-H. Freeman.

Barbercheck, M. (2001). *Mixed messages: Men and women in advertisements in science.* In M. Barbercheck, D. Geisman, H. O. Ozttirk, & M. Wayne (Eds.), *Women, science, and technology: A reader in feminist science studies.* New York, NY: Routledge.

Brickhouse, N., Lowery, P., & Schultz, K. (2000). What kind of girl does science? The construction of school science identities. *Journal of Research in Science Teaching, 37*(5), 441–458. https://doi.org/10.1002/(SICI)1098-2736(200005)37:5<441::AID-TEA4>3.0.CO;2-3

Buzzetto-More, N., Ukoha, O., & Rustagi, N. (2010). Unlocking the barriers to women and minorities in computer science and information systems studies: Results from a multi-methodological study conducted at two minority-serving institutions. *Journal of Information Technology Education, 9,* 115–131.

Buchanan, N. T., Settles, I. H., Hall, A. T., & O'Connor, R. C. (2014). Organizational strategies for reducing and confronting sexual harassment. *Journal of Social Issues (Special Issue on Confronting and Reducing Sexism)*.

Burke, P., & Stets, E. (2009). *Identity theory.* New York, NY: Oxford University Press.

Byars-Winston, A. M., Estrada, Y. E., Howard, C. H., Davis, D., & Zalapa, J. (2010). Influence of social cognitive and ethnic variables on academic goals of underrepresented students in science and engineering. *Journal of Counseling Psychology, 57*(2), 205–218.

Byers-Winston, A., Rogers, J., Branchaw, J., Pribbenow, C., Hanke, R., & Pfund, C. (2016). New measures assessing predictors of academic persistence for historically underrepresented racial/ethnic undergraduates in science. *Life Sciences Education, 15*(3), 1–11.

Carlone, H. B., & Johnson, A. C. (2007). Understanding the science experiences of successful women of color: Science identity as an analytic lens. *Journal of Research Teaching, 44*(8), 1187–1218.

Cech, E., Rubineau, B., Silbey, S., & Seron, C. (2011). Professional role confidence and gendered persistence in engineering. *American Sociological Review, 76*(5), 641–666.

Charleston, L., Adserias, R. M., Lang, N., & Jackson, J. (2014). Intersectionality and STEM: The Role of Race and Gender in the Academic Pursuits of African American Women in STEM. *Journal of Management Policy and Practice, 2,* 17–37.

Dawn, A. (2013). Family matters: familial support and science identity formation for African American female STEM majors. Retrieved from https://eric.ed.gov/?id=ED560384

De Welde, K., & Laursen, S. (2011). The glass obstacle course: Informal and formal barriers for women Ph.D. students in STEM fields. Retrieved from http://genderandset.open.ac.uk/index.php/genderandset/article/viewFile/205/363

Diekman, A. B., & Steinberg, M. (2013). Navigating social roles in pursuit of important goals: A communal goal congruity account of STEM pursuits. *Social & Personality Psychology Compass, 7*(7), 487–501. http://dx.doi.org/10.1111/spc3.12042

Espinosa, L. L. (2008). The academic self-concept of African American and Latina(o) men and women in STEM majors. *Journal of Women and Minorities in Science and Engineering, 14*(2), 177–203.

Farinde, A., & Lewis, C. (2012). The underrepresentation of African American female students in STEM fields: Implication for classroom teachers. *US-China Education Review, 2*(4), 421–430.

Farkas, T., & Leaper, C. (2016). Chivalry's double-edged sword: how girls' and boys' paternalistic attitudes relate to their possible family and work selves. *Sex Roles, 74,* 220–230. doi:10.1007/s11199-015-0556

Federal Glass Ceiling Commission. (1995). A solid investment: Making full use of the nation's human capital. Recommendations of the Federal Glass Ceiling Commission. Retrieved from https://www.dol.gov/oasam/programs/history/reich/reports/ceiling2.pdf

142   A. BOOKER

Fisk, S., Cuddy, A., Glick, P., & Xu, J. (2002). A model (often mixed) stereotype content: Competence and warmth respectively follow from status and competition. *Journal of Personality and Social Psychology, 82*, 878–902.

Garbee, E. (2017). The problem with the "pipeline": A pervasive metaphor in STEM education has some serious flaws. Retrieved from http://www.slate.com/technology/2018/07/russia-election-hacking-muellers-latest-indictment-suggests-it-could-be-even-more-damaging-next-time.html

George, Y. S., Neale, D. S., Van Horne, V., & Malcolm, S. M. (2001). In pursuit of a diverse science, technology, engineering, and mathematics workforce. Washington, DC: American Association for the Advancement of Science. Retrieved from http://ehrweb.aaas.org/mge/Reports/Report1/AGEP/?downloadURL=true&loId=EB79A2C2-3280-4404-AAF3-0D5D3F8A9D6D

Herrera, F. A., Hurtado, S., Garcia, G. A., & Gasiewski, J. (2012, April). A model for redefining STEM identity for talented STEM graduate students. *Paper Presented at the American Educational Research Association Annual Conference*, Vancouver, BC.

Jackson, J. L., & Charleston, L. (2012). *Differential gender outcomes of career exploration* sessions for African American undergraduates: An examination of a computing science *outreach effort at predominantly White institutions*. In C. R. Chambers & R. V. Sharpe (Eds.), *Black female undergraduates on campus: Successes and challenges* (pp. 185–197). Bingley, England: Emerald Group Publishing.

Johnson, A. C., Brown, J., Carlone, H., & Cuevas, A. K. (2011). Authoring identity amidst the treacherous terrain of science: A multiracial feminist examination of the journeys of three women of color in science. *Journal of Research in Science Teaching, 48*(4), 339–366. doi:10.1002/tea.20411

Jones, S. R., & McEwen, M. K. (2000). A conceptual model of multiple dimensions of identity. *Journal of College Student Development, 41*, 405–414.

Ko, L., Kachchaf, R., Ong, M., & Hodari, A. (2013). Narratives of the double bind: Intersectionality in life stories of women of color in physics, astrophysics, and astronomy. *AIP Conference Proceedings, 1513*(1), 222–225.

Margolis, J., Goode, J., & Bernier, D. (2011). The need for computer science. *Educational Leadership, 68*(5), 68–72.

Lane, K. A., Goh, J. X., & Driver-Linn, E. (2012). Implicit science stereotypes mediate the relationship between gender and academic participation. *Sex Roles: A Journal of Research, 66*(3–4), 220–234

Miner, K., Settles, I. H., Pratt-Hyatt, J., & Brady, C. (2012). Experiencing incivility in organizations: The buffering effects of emotional and organizational support. *Journal of Applied Social Psychology, 42*(2), 340–372.

O'Brien, L., Blodorn, A., Adams, G., Garcia, D., & Hammer, E. (2014). Ethnic variation in gender-STEM stereotypes and STEM participation: An intersectional approach. *Cultural Diversity and Ethnic Minority Psychology*. Retrieved from http://www.apa.org/news/press/releases/2014/09/women-stem-majors.aspx

Ong, M., Wright, C. Espinosa, L., & Orfield, G. (2011). Inside the double-blind: A synthesis of empirical research on undergraduate and graduate women of color in science, technology, engineering, and mathematics. *Harvard Educational Review, 81*(2), 172–209.

Parker, A. (2013). Family matters: Familial support and science identity formation for African American female STEM majors. Retrieved from https://eric.ed.gov/?id=ED560384

Perez, T., Cromley, J., & Kaplan, A. (2014). The role of identity development, values, and costs in college STEM retention. *Journal of Educational Psychology, 106*(1), 315–329.

Riegle-Crumb, C., King, B., Grodsky, E., & Muller, C. (2012). The more things change, the more they stay the same? Prior achievement fails to explain gender inequality in entry into STEM college majors over time. *American Educational Research Journal, 49*(6), 1048–1073.

Riegle-Crumb, C., Moore, C., & Ramos-Wada, A. (2011). Who wants to have a career in science or math? Exploring adolescents' future aspirations by gender and race/ethnicity. *Science Education, 95*, 458–476.

Robnett, R. D., & Leaper, C. (2013). Friendship groups, personal motivation, and gender in relation to high school students' STEM career interest. *Journal of Research on Adolescence, 23*(4), 652–664.

Science, Technology, Engineering, and Math: Education for Global Leadership. (2015). U.S. Department of Education. Retrieved from https://www.ed.gov/stem

Settles, I. (2014). Women in STEAM: Challenges and determinants of success and well-being. *Psychological Science Agenda. American Psychological Association.* Retrieved July 31, 2018, from http://www.apa.org/science/about/psa/2014/10/women-STEAM.aspx

Settles, I. H., Cortina, L. M., Buchanan, N. T., & Miner, K. (2013). Derogation, discrimination, and (dis)satisfaction with jobs in science: A gendered analysis. *Psychology of Women Quarterly, 37*(2), 179–191.

Sheehy, K. (2012). Minorities need STEM role models too. Retrieved from https://www.usnews.com/news/blogs/stem-education/2012/06/28/minorities-need-stem-role-models-too

Shih, M., Pittinsky, T. L., & Ambady, N. (1999). Stereotype susceptibility: Identity salience and shifts in quantitative performance. *Psychological Science, 10*, 80–83.

Steinke, J. (2017). Adolescent girls' STEM identity formation and media images of STEM professionals: Considering the influence of contextual cues. *Frontiers in Psychology, 8*, 716. Retrieved from https://www.frontiersin.org/article/10.3389/fpsyg.2017.00716

Syed, M., & Chemers, M. M. (2011). Ethnic minorities and women in STEM: Casting a wide net to address a persistent social problem. *Journal of Social Issues, 67*(3), 435–441.

Wang, X. (2013). Why students choose STEM majors motivation, high school learning, and postsecondary context of support. *American Education Research Journal, 50*(5), 1081–1121.

Williams, J., Phillips, K., & Hall, E. (2014). Double jeopardy? Gender bias against women of color in science. Retrieved from http://www.uchastings.edu/news/articles/2015/01/double-jeopardy-report.pdf

AFTERWORD

CHAPTER 9

STRENGTHENING IDENTITIES TO COMBAT MARGINALIZATION

Recurring Themes and Implications

Stephen D. Hancock and Sonyia C. Richardson
University of North Carolina, Charlotte

"Do not let others define who you are. Define yourself. Do not be limited by what others expect of you, but reach confidently for the stars"

—Shirley Ann Jackson

INTRODUCTION

As a scientist, national leader, and university president, Jackson's quote is deeply rooted in the intellectual, sociocultural, gendered, and racial intersectionalities that have shaped her as a preeminent physicist. Because her work has revolutionized how we live, think, and function, this quote has direct significance for this book. In these three sections *Socialization, Mentoring,* and *Identity*, Jackson's quote is reverberated with astounding

Seeing The HiddEn Minority, pp. 147–152
Copyright © 2020 by Information Age Publishing
All rights of reproduction in any form reserved.

148 S. D. HANCOCK and S. C. RICHARDSON

clarity that African American people must define themselves as STEM professionals and combat the limitations and low expectations of the curriculum, teachers, and society. In this concluding chapter we explore the recurring theme of identity and how the self is defined. The notion of defining self is an important concept if African American students are to nurture an identity as STEM professionals. However, defining self is not easy or static, nor is it an isolated phenomenon. Defining self requires a sense of sociocultural and historical knowledge. We use the chapters of this book to examine ways to define self. We also explore how to be liberated from the marginalizing impact of low expectations and limitations to STEM education and careers. Marginalization of African American students in STEM is an endemic reality in schools. As a result, efforts to combat low expectations and limitations through mentoring and anti-biased curriculum are discussed in this section. Further, we consider the implications of removing barriers and equitably supporting African American students STEM goals. Finally, we propose future research that will support knowledge and practice for nurturing STEM professionals and combatting marginalization.

STRENGTHENING IDENTITIES: I AM BECAUSE THEY ARE!

Defining self is a major theme that transcends the chapters in this book. However, defining self as an African American STEM professional is problematic in hegemonic systems of resistance. The hegemonic systems that resist the positive development of STEM identities for African American students are grounded in societal marginalization and adverse curriculum content. The challenge that many African American students face in developing positive STEM identities are often sourced in the social marginalization of race. Early in life children form in-group and out-group associations, knowledge, and beliefs based on race. These beliefs are reified through societal images, customs, portrayals, and perceptions that demean and marginalize African American culture. Consequently, African American students and adults must navigate societal marginalization that unjustly describe us as having low intelligence, low work ethic, delinquent, and a host of other labels. In addition to societal marginalization, we must also transverse the negative impact of the STEM curriculum on identity development. The curriculum is arguably the most important abiotic element in the school ecosystem. As such it has the power to promote a set of beliefs, values, and content that are deemed important and superior to all omitted knowledge. Unfortunately, neither the K–12 nor the general college curriculum support multiple perspectives on STEM achievements that combat the hegemonic system of whiteness as superior.

In an effort to strengthen STEM identities it is important that African American students not define themselves through the eyes of "them" or the hegemonic resistance to African American success. Rather, STEM identities must be defined through the eyes of the historical and important accomplishment of African American scientists, inventors, engineers, and mathematicians. In an effort to strengthen African American STEM identities the curriculum must equitably include the achievements of all cultures, races, and gender that contributed to STEM accomplishments. A focus on self-efficacy that is nurtured through the accomplishments of African American STEM professionals must be present in the K–12 and college curriculum. Lastly, in an effort to strengthen STEM identities for African American students the stories of STEM innovators must be shared in homes, churches, and communities.

COMBATTING MARGINALIZATION: IF I CAN'T WORK WITH YOU, I WILL WORK AROUND YOU

Another theme that permeates the chapters in this book centers on resisting marginalization and its impact on positive STEM identity development. The legacy of the marginalization of African American students in the STEM field and resulting effects, including their underrepresentation and exclusion, have been researched extensively (Lundy-Wagner, 2013; Perna et al., 2009). While solutions are provided for addressing these inequities, a constantly recurring theme centers on the establishment of a science identity. These identities need to remain steadfast through resistance and marginalization. Along the same lines, the perseverance of African American students within the STEM field should not be relegated to students who are able to "buck the trend" and resist dropout (Archer, Dewitt, & Osborne, 2015). Rather, acceptance of this science identity aids needs to be normalized, reinforced, and supported. Annie Easley, an African American female computer scientist, rocket scientist, and mathematician, once stated that "If I can't work with you, I will work around you" (NASA, 2015, para. 2). In other words, the STEM identity needs to be personally affirmed and students must not allow systems to deter them towards non-STEM fields and careers. Moreover, systems including family members, community centers, local gyms, churches, and fraternity or sorority groups must equip and sustain them through these fields and assist with their socialization in STEM.

Mentors, faculty, and universities need to acknowledge that African American students who maintain a commitment to the STEM field are oftentimes required to work around barriers. These networks of support can overpower the structural barriers that students face if there is a commitment

150   S. D. HANCOCK and S. C. RICHARDSON

to reimagining policies and structures. Unfortunately, until these barriers become dismantled, the work will be exhausting and difficult. Thus, the role of these supports becomes even more instrumental in helping them to maintain their tenacity and dedication towards the field. As stated by Christine Darden, African American Aeronautical Engineer for NASA, "I was able to stand on the shoulders of those women who came before me, and women who came after me were able to stand on mine" (NASA, 2013, para. 23). Accordingly, combatting marginalization requires a working around existing barriers and standing on the shoulders of supports both past and present.

IMPLICATIONS: DO NOT ALLOW YOUR MIND TO BE IMPRISONED BY MAJORITY THINKING

Seeing The HiddEn Minority examined challenges that African American students face in STEM, particularly as it pertains to socialization, mentoring, and identity development. Socialization strategies focused on using frameworks of socialization and acculturation and ecological systems theory. Mentoring based strategies affirmed STEM advocacy, mentorship support in historically Black colleges and universities versus predominantly White institutions, and student support networks. From an identity perspective, strategies included reshaping the pipeline, combatting curriculum identity trauma, and countering a distorted science identity. Collectively, these strategies are aimed at exposing the barriers while endorsing potential solutions.

Overall implications from this work reinforce the need to develop STEM curricular that centers African American innovators, scientists, and engineers both present and past. It acknowledges the historical and contemporary contributions of African American STEM professionals who are often excluded. The inclusion of these scholars helps to reinforce African American STEM identities for students in general. As stated eloquently by Patricia Bath, African American female ophthalmologist, "Do not allow your mind to be imprisoned by majority thinking" (Davidson, 2005, para. 3). Helping African American STEM students to break free from this imprisonment requires an altering of curricular that continuously reinforces the dominant narrative at the K–12 and higher education level.

In addition to positioning STEM curricular to become more culturally inclusive, efforts need to be implemented to provide academic, social, cultural, and emotional mentoring for African American STEM students. To guide these efforts, the recruitment of underrepresented faculty and staff within STEM departments is necessary. These individuals are more likely to align with the values and experiences of diverse STEM scholars and meet their needs (Hayes & Bigler, 2013).

CONCLUSION

Each chapter in this book posits themes that include identity and culture, navigating hurdles in graduate programs, developing mentors to support STEM students, and reconstructing curriculum that include the STEM accomplishments of all. While there is no panacea to solve the complex challenge of supporting African American students who are interested in STEM professions, the work must begin with both practical and research solutions. Practical solutions include curriculum reconstruction that equitably include African American STEM innovations as well as combatting the societal ideals, beliefs, and images that negatively depict the African American culture. Research solution might include conducting an ethnographic study on African American STEM students and professionals to investigate their pathways, success, failures, and challenges from K–12 to career.

Nonetheless, if African American students are to define themselves in an environment where "white privilege and power impinge upon the construction of racialized imageries and knowledges used to legitimate a racist social order" (Escayg, 2019, p. 8), then they must learn and share the imageries and knowledge of African American STEM pioneers that resisted and moved beyond the racial social order to accomplish greatness.

REFERENCES

Archer, L., Dewitt, J., & Osborne, J. (2015). Is science for us? Black students' and parents' views of science and science careers. *Science Education, 99*(2), 199–237. doi:10.1002/sce.21146

Davidson, M. (2005). *Innovative lives: The right to sight: Patricia Bath.* Retrieved from https://invention.si.edu/innovative-lives-right-sight-patricia-bath

Escayg, K. (2019). "Who's got the power?": A critical examination of the anti-bias curriculum. *International Journal of Child Care and Education Policy, 13*(6), 1–18.

Hayes, A. R., & Bigler, R. S. (2013). Gender-related values, perceptions of discrimination, and mentoring in STEM graduate training. *International Journal of Gender, Science and Technology, 5*(3), 255–280. Retrieved from http://genderandset.open.ac.uk/index.php/genderandset/article/view/403>

Lundy-Wagner, V. C. (2013). Is it really a man's world? Black men in science, technology, engineering, and mathematics at historically Black colleges and universities. *The Journal of Negro Education, 82*(2), 157–168. doi:10.7709/jnegroeducation.82.2.0157

NASA. (2013). *Standing on the shoulders of a computer.* Retrieved from https://www.nasa.gov/centers/langley/news/researchernews/rn_CDarden.html

NASA. (2015). *Annie Easley, computer scientist.* Retrieved from https://www.nasa.gov/feature/annie-easley-computer-scientist

Perna, L., Lundy-Wagner, V., Drezner, N. D., Gasman, M., Yoon, S., Bose, E., & Gary, S. (2009). The contributions of HBCUs to the preparation of African American women for STEM careers: A case study. *Research in Higher Education, 50*(1), 1–23. doi:10.1007/s11162-008-9110-y

ABOUT THE CONTRIBUTORS

Daniel Mason Alston, is an Assistant Professor of Elementary Science Education at the University of North Carolina at Charlotte and a graduate of Clemson University. His scholarship examines the development and impact of student-centered teaching methods such as, inquiry-based and STEM instruction. He also seeks to better understand the various person variables, which impact teacher enactment and persistence in student-centered teaching methods. Currently, he is working on a grant-funded project studying the holistic development of STEM faculty at various institution types.

Ansley Booker is the Director of the Mercer University Educational Opportunity Center (TRiO Programs) and an adjunct professor. She attended Georgia Southern University where she earned a Bachelor of Arts degree in biology. In 2007, she was selected for the Ronald E. McNair Postbaccalaureate Achievement Program. She earned a Master of Science degree from the University of Georgia in pharmacy with certificates in clinical trials and regulatory affairs. In 2016, she was awarded Georgia Southern University's 40 under 40 Alumni Award as well as the STAR Award from Mercer University's Student Affairs Division in 2017. Ansley completed her doctoral studies at Mercer University in the Higher Education Leadership program. Her dissertation focused on African American women who have obtained STEM graduate degrees in computer science, engineering or physical science. Her goal was to unearth barriers and catalysts to their graduate and career success in order to develop retention models that may improve the college persistence of women and minority students in STEM disciplines.

154 ABOUT the CONTRIBUTORS

Lenora Crabtree is a part-time faculty member for the University Honors Program and Department of Biological Sciences at the University of North Carolina at Charlotte. In addition, she is a doctoral student in Curriculum and Instruction, Urban Education specialization at UNCC. She possesses a Masters degree in Biological Sciences (UNCC) and a Bachelor of Science in Molecular Biology (Vanderbilt University). Her teaching experience includes 16 years as a high school Biology and Chemistry teacher. Her research interests include encouraging the use of critical pedagogies in STEM education and the impact of gifted education disproportionality on student preparation for STEM majors.

Cameron D. Denson is an Associate Professor of Technology, Engineering and Design Education at North Carolina State University in Raleigh, N.C. His work in Science, Technology, Engineering, and Mathematics (STEM) Education is focused on informal learning environments (particularly mentoring) and their impact on underrepresented students' self-efficacy and motivation as it pertains to engineering. His research efforts have also focused on the integration of engineering design into high school curriculums and how this would create pathways to technical careers for underrepresented populations.

Letimicia Fears currently a teaching postdoctoral fellowship in the Vanderbilt University Center for Science Outreach, which includes bringing interdisciplinary, research-centered learning experiences to public school students. Letimicia works closely with teachers to plan Problem or Phenomenon Based Learning projects, make STEM career connections and engage the students in exciting hands-on science experiences. This fellowship allows her to teach real world science to middle school students where she can focus on encouraging the next generation of STEM professionals and business people. Her long-term goal is to increase diversity in STEM by mentoring students and engaging in STEM education and research at the K–12 level.

Stephen D. Hancock is an Associate Professor of Multicultural Education in the Department of Reading and Elementary Education at UNC Charlotte where he also serves as the Assistant Director of the Urban Education Collaborative. He served as an International Visiting Professor at the Pedagogische Hocshule in Ludwigsburg, and as a delegate to Mexico, China, Singapore, Malaysia, and England where he has worked to provide study abroad experiences for teachers and students.

Karri A. Holley is Professor of Higher Education at The University of Alabama. She earned a PhD and MEd from the University of Southern

California, and a BA from The University of Alabama. Her research interests include organizational change in higher education, graduate and doctoral education, interdisciplinarity, and qualitative inquiry. She currently serves as editor of *Studies in Graduate and Postdoctoral Education*. Her articles have been included in *Educational Researcher, Higher Education, Innovative Higher Education, Journal of Diversity in Higher Education, Studies in Higher Education,* and *Journal of Higher Education*. She previously worked in admissions for the Grazadio School of Business at Pepperdine University, and also served as a Peace Corps Volunteer in Ukraine.

Tamecia R. Jones is an Assistant Professor of Technology, Engineering and Design Education at North Carolina State University in Raleigh, NC. She conducts research to develop assessment tools for informal and formal K–12 settings, using innovative strategies to conduct unobtrusive assessment.

Joretta Joseph has a Doctorate from the University of Southern California, a MBA from Howard University, and BA from Clark Atlanta University. She has worked extensively with minority doctoral students enrolled in STEM disciplines. Her research looks at various issues of diversity and equity in higher education. Specifically, her research interests include campus culture, student success, institutional effectiveness, and issues of equity, as presented in her dissertation and recent publication. She also serves as a board member for a charter school that serves students in grades K–8, and has traveled internationally to focus on issues of equity and diversity. She is also a community advocate that believes in empowering girls and eliminating racism. She is a published scholar on issues of equity in science and throughout higher education.

Brandi Copeland-Kamp is a doctoral student at Clemson University and an adjunct faculty at the University of North Caroline at Charlotte. Her research agenda stems from social justice reform and the ways educational policies can have an unequal or adverse effect on the needs of marginalized populations. She is passionate about STEM and believes that every person can be positively impacted though the understanding of the nature of science and its tenets and that through this understanding, a more just society may develop. As a result, she is devoted to finding instructional strategies that impart that knowledge best. Further, she believes that technology has the potential to overcome barriers that have prevented certain groups from accessing all parts of school culture in the past by changing the ways that school is conceived.

156 ABOUT the CONTRIBUTORS

Carrie Klein is a PhD Candidate and Research Assistant in the Higher Education Program at George Mason University. Her research interests are rooted in understanding and interrogating the social and structural inequities that exist in higher education systems. Her work exists at the intersection of organizational structure, power, and privilege and recent projects have focused on the impacts of big data, the structural challenges faced by women and historically underrepresented students, and the collaborative practices of culturally disparate organizational groups within higher education.

Monica Miles has recently been named as the associate director of University at Buffalo's Great Lakes Program and the Coastal Literacy Specialist through a joint appointment between UB, New York Sea Grant and Cornell University's College of Agriculture and Life Sciences. She earned a doctorate from the Curriculum, Instruction and the Science of Learning Program in UB's Graduate School of Education, with a concentration in science education in 2017. Monica's research focuses on the role of identity, racialized experiences, and marginalization in K–12 and higher STEM spaces. She seeks to promote solutions for creating inclusive STEM environments for underrepresented students and boldly challenges systems of oppression. Monica maintains a commitment to social justice efforts through critical examinations of society and education.

Hironao Okahana is Associate Vice President, Research and Policy Analysis at the Council of Graduate Schools (CGS). He studies master's and doctoral education with particular emphasis on enrollment trends, diversity and inclusiveness, as well as, career pathways and labor market outcomes. At CGS, he directs various research projects and has authored and co-authored a number of technical reports, research briefs, commissioned papers, and peer-reviewed articles. Okahana earned his PhD in Higher Education and Organizational Change and MPP in public policy from University of California, Los Angeles, and his undergraduate degrees from California State University, Long Beach. In addition, he is a Higher Education Program Affiliate and Adjunct Faculty at George Mason University in Fairfax, VA.

Michelle B. Pass is a Senior Lecturer and Laboratory Director in the Department of Biological Sciences at the University of North Carolina at Charlotte, and a PhD Student in Curriculum & Instruction, Urban Education at the University of North Carolina at Charlotte. Her areas of interest are persistence and attrition of underrepresented groups in biological sciences, self-efficacy and science identity among underrepre-

About the Contributors 157

sented minority STEM majors, and higher education access, engagement, and success, particularly for underrepresented minority students.

Sonyia C. Richardson is the Undergraduate Program Director and Clinical Assistant Professor in the School of Social Work at UNC Charlotte. She possesses a master's degree in Social Work (University of North Carolina Chapel Hill) and a Bachelor of Arts in Psychology (University of North Carolina Charlotte). Additionally, she is a PhD candidate in the Curriculum and Instruction, Urban Education specialization (University of North Carolina Charlotte). She addresses the intersection of social work and urban education in addressing systemic educational issues.

Andrea L. Tyler is the Director of Graduate Students Services and a Research Associate at Tennessee State University. Andrea earned her doctoral degree in Educational Leadership (Curriculum and Cultural Studies) from the Miami University of Ohio. She also holds a master's degree in Curriculum and Instruction (STEM Education) and a bachelors degree in Mechanical Engineering. Her research foci include the experiences of Blacks in higher education, specifically graduate students and pretenure faculty in Science and Engineering. These interests have led her to conduct research on a variety of topics such as the influence of mentoring relationships and social interactions; race/gender/class equity in STEM, identity formations and stereotype bias; and graduate student outcomes and career choices.